DECORATIVE PAINTING

Aileen Bratton

DECORATIVE PAINTING
TREASURES

NORTH LIGHT BOOKS
CINCINNATI, OHIO

About the Author

Aileen Bratton has been involved in decorative art for some twenty-five years. Teaching and traveling throughout the world provides her the opportunity to share her knowledge and love of painting. She is a Certified Decorative Artist (CDA) of the Society of Decorative Painters, passing the floral part of her Master Decorative Artist degree in 1980. Aileen has served the society and decorative painting in many different ways, including in the elected positions of board member and president of the society. She was the recipient of the society's Dedicated Service Award in 1986 and was honored with the President's Commendation Award at the 1991 national convention in Kansas City, for her outstanding contributions toward the promotion and recognition of decorative painting beyond the boundaries of the society.

Aileen is the author of ten books and six instructional videos that are very popular due to her detailed, easy-to-understand method of teaching. This volume contains the best of the projects from Aileen's previous books now out of print.

Aileen enjoys all the different aspects of designing and painting, but most of all she loves watching beginning painters become turned on to decorative painting and watching their skills expand. The excitement of sparking their imagination and creativity provides the motivation to keep her striving to improve her teaching skills and develop new ways to present the concepts of decorative painting. ✒

Aileen Bratton's Decorative Painting Treasures. Copyright © 1998 by North Light Books. Manufactured in China. All rights reserved. No part of this book may be reproduced in any form or by any electronic or mechanical means including information storage and retrieval systems without permission in writing from the publisher, except by a reviewer, who may quote brief passages in a review. Published by North Light Books, an imprint of F&W Publications, Inc., 1507 Dana Avenue, Cincinnati, Ohio 45207. (800) 289-0963. First edition.

Other fine North Light Books are available from your local bookstore, art supply store or direct from the publisher.

02   01   00   99   98   5   4   3   2   1

Library of Congress Cataloging-in-Publication Data

Bratton, Aileen.
    Aileen Bratton's decorative painting treasures / by Aileen Bratton.—1st ed.
        p.   cm.
    Includes index.
    ISBN 0-89134-871-9 (pb : alk. paper)
    1. Painting. 2. Decoration and ornament. 3. Flowers in art. 4. Plants in art. I. Title. II Title: Decorative painting treasures
TT385.B73   1998
745.7'23—dc21   97-43101
                                                                                                            CIP

Content edited by Jennifer Long
Production edited by Bob Beckstead
Interior designed by Sandy Kent
Cover designed by Clare Finney

Amanda

Garrison

Lisa

Dedication

The only thing that has been more important or has brought greater joy and love to me than my painting has been my family. I want to dedicate this book to my three wonderful grandchildren: Amanda Lee, Lisa Nicole and Garrison Kyle. They are such a blessing to my husband and me. We have so many wonderful times with them and such memories to treasure.

Table of Contents

Potpourri Pansies, page 70

Poppies and Grapes, page 86

Poppin' Peaches, page 91

Lilies and Lace, page 108

Gathering Your Supplies

I wish everyone could be exposed to tole and decorative painting because my life has been greatly enriched since Mary Jo Leisure convinced me, many years ago, that she could teach me to paint. It seems strange to me that people seldom say, "I can't play the piano; I have no talent." Most people assume that with study and practice, they can learn to play the piano, at least well enough to bring pleasure and to provide an enjoyable pastime. Painting is no different. Anyone can learn to paint who has the sincere desire to do so. The difference between those who do and those who don't is not talent, it's desire.

In addition to the pleasures of painting, there is also a tangible product. Amateur paintings may not challenge the classics, but they are the results of a creative effort and can be the source of much pride. Original paintings in the home add individuality and say "interesting people live here!" There are so many special touches you can add to your home with your own decorative art. Just think of the joy your family and friends will feel when you give them a gift you have created, one that truly comes from the heart.

Paints

I used a mixed palette of oils and alkyds to create these designs. One of the main differences between the two mediums is the drying time. The alkyds will be completely dry in eighteen hours, while the oils will take much longer. The alkyd pigments are placed in a binder of alcohol and acids or oil-modified alkyd resin, and therefore dry much faster than the vegetable oil binders used in oil paints.

Alkyds are also more transparent than oils, making them nice for glazing and staining. Titanium White in oils is an opaque color, but Titanium White in alkyd is more transparent, so it will not overwhelm or become murky as fast as Titanium White oil when added to weaker, more transparent colors or when overblended. By using alkyd Titanium White and some of the slower-drying colors (such as the yellows and reds) with the remainder of the palette in oils, my paintings will easily be dry in eighteen hours.

This mixed palette works very well.

The alkyds are applied with pressure to the surface just like oils, except that they dry more quickly when pulled out on the palette in loading the brush. Your color mixes will have to be mixed again and again, but this is desirable because it helps give variation in the painting.

Start a fresh palette several times during each day when using the alkyds and clean your brushes as soon as you finish painting. If painting with an entire palette of alkyds, you will

Palette

Winsor & Newton Oils	Winsor & Newton Alkyds	
Alizarin Crimson	Alizarin Crimson	AC
Ivory Black	Ivory Black	Blk
Burnt Sienna	Burnt Sienna	BS
Burnt Umber	Burnt Umber	BU
Copper	Use oil color	C
Cadmium Green Pale	Use oil color	CGP
Cadmium Lemon	Cadmium Lemon	CL
Cadmium Yellow Deep	Cadmium Orange	CO
Cadmium Red Deep	Cadmium Red Deep	CRD
Cadmium Scarlet	Cadmium Red Light	CRL
Bright Red	Cadmium Red Medium	CRM
Cadmium Yellow	Cadmium Yellow Deep	CYD
Aurora Yellow	Cadmium Yellow Light	CYL
Cadmium Yellow Pale	Cadmium Yellow Medium	CYM
Dioxazine Purple	Dioxazine Purple	DP
Ultramarine Blue	French Ultramarine	FU
Gold	Use oil color	G
Indian Red	Indian Red	IR
Naples Yellow	Naples Yellow Hue	NYH
Oxide of Chromium	Use oil color	OC
Prussian Blue	Prussian Blue	PB
Payne's Gray	Payne's Gray	PG
Renaissance Gold	Use oil color	RG
Raw Sienna	Raw Sienna	RS
Raw Umber	Raw Umber	RU
Viridian Green	Viridian Green	VG
Titanium White	Titanium White	W
Yellow Ochre	Yellow Ochre	YO

Rembrandt Oils		
Burnt Carmine	BC	
Brownish Madder	BM	
King's Blue	KB	
Naples Yellow Light Extra	NYL	
Naples Yellow Reddish Extra	NYR	
Warm Gray	WG	

In the color setups, oil colors were only used when the alkyd color was not available.

need to adjust your painting procedure by completing one element before moving to another element. As the paint dries it is more difficult to add stronger highlights and darker shading without pulling holes in the painting. If the paint should become dry and sticky, tending to pull holes, just pick up fresh paint from the palette and use pressure on the brush to work back into the semidry area. It will become workable again. If you are applying a finish to a mixed painting of alkyds and oils, wait as long as possible to allow it to dry evenly, then spray lightly over the top of the painting, not directly *at* the painting. The paint has a tendency to crackle or bubble due to the difference in drying speed of the paints.

Brushes

Your painting will only be as good as the brushes you are using. Decorative art requires good brushes with sharp chisel edges. My brushes are the most important equipment I own. To blend the way I do, you must use a short bristle brush (a bright) because the longer bristle brush will not snap back fast enough, causing it to drag through your paint. I recommend four flat brushes for beginners: no. 2, no. 4, no. 6 and no. 8. I use Winsor & Newton series #710 brushes. These are red sable brushes consisting of very high quality red sable bristles. I don't recommend the synthetic flats because they aren't soft and resilient enough to snap back. In fact, with alkyds they become limp. Also, if they aren't cared for properly, the edges will curl. To prevent this, use only mineral spirits to rinse your brushes.

In addition to the bright and flats, you should have a liner brush that will produce the best linework with the least amount of frustration. The liner brush I recommend is a Winsor & Newton series 3A, no. 00. Good, less-expensive synthetic liners are Loew Cornell, series 801, no. 00; Robert Simmons, series 161, no. 10/0; and Marxbrush, series 865, no. 10/0.

Care of Brushes

Your brushes are the most important and expensive equipment you own, so take care of them. Treat your brushes as you would your children—with tender loving care!

Dry wipe your brushes carefully using a soft, lint-free paper towel or other cloth that isn't stiff or rough. I fold my paper towels into fourths. To dry wipe, place your brush between the layers of towel and press with your index finger. You'll remove more paint this way than you will by wiping the brush across the towel. This also results in less destruction of the brush, particularly the chisel edge.

If the corners of your brushes show wear, you're not painting on the flat of the brush. I would suggest painting with a brush one size smaller to correct this problem.

Clean the brush in good, odorless, mineral spirit-based brush cleaner at the end of each painting session. Other cleaners will cause damage to the brush. For rinsing brushes, I prefer the Better Way jars, which contain sponges with fuzzy hair. The metal coils in some jars damage the bristles of the brush quickly. I clean my brushes by placing a squirt of Winsor & Newton's Art Gel and a squirt of lard oil side by side on my palette. (Don't use the oil if cleaning synthetic brushes as they will become limp.) After rinsing the brush, load it with lard oil and work the brush gently back and forth in the Art Gel. Dry wipe often and repeat until the brush is clean, leaving no signs of color on the cloth. Leave a little of the mixture in the brush to shape and protect it. Be certain you follow the instructions for use if you use other brands of cleaners. Watch your sable brushes—too much of some soaps will cause them to become limp.

Store the brushes in an upright container or brush bag where the bristles of the brush are undisturbed. Rinse the brushes in odorless cleaner before you begin to paint again.

Basic Supplies
- Paints
- Brushes
- Paper towels
- Disposable parchment palette pad
- Sanador odorless brush cleaner (or other mineral spirit-based cleaner)
- Medium (Winsor & Newton Blending and Glazing Medium)
- Palette knife
- Lard oil and Art Gel

Transferring, Preparation and Finishing Supplies
- Tracing paper
- Pilot pen
- Graphite transfer paper
- Stylus
- Soft eraser
- Wood sealer
- Sandpaper
- Tack cloth
- Varnish
- Krylon Matte spray, #1311
- Basecoat paint (acrylic, alkyd or oil)

Optional Supplies
- Brush holder
- Palette keeper
- Better Way jar
- Clipboard, pencil and notebook

Background Preparation

Preparing Wood

Fill any holes or scratches with a good wood filler that will take stain. Sand with the grain of the wood using #150 sandpaper. Wipe with a tack cloth. Seal all wood surfaces with a good wood sealer, such as Designs From the Heart Wood Sealer—this is a lacquer-base sealer and will be dry and ready for the next step in thirty minutes. Seal both the front and back. If the surface is rough, sand with #400 or #600 wet-and-dry sandpaper, but don't get the surface too slick. With the exception of glass, the final step before applying the pattern to all surfaces is a light spray of Krylon Matte #1311.

Staining

Apply a very light wash of oil or alkyd color thinned with turpentine. The most common staining color is Burnt Umber, but any color may be used. Using a soft rag, rub with the grain. Let dry and spray lightly with Krylon Matte #1311, then deepen the edges and corners with a darker color. If a medium is needed, use paint thinner, linseed oil or Blending and Glazing Medium (Winsor & Newton).

Painting and Antiquing

Apply several thin coats of acrylic basecoat, going with the grain of the wood. Allow the paint to dry well between coats. Sand gently between coats with #400 or #600 wet-and-dry sandpaper. For an acrylic wash, one light coat of paint—which may be thinned with water—is applied to the surface, going with the grain of the wood.

Before antiquing, spray with Krylon Matte #1311. Pick up turpentine and an earth color, such as Raw Sienna or Burnt Umber, on a lint-free cloth. Too much turpentine will cause your paint to dry too fast, and too much paint will make it sticky. When this is dry, spray lightly and deepen your antiquing once more.

Flecking or Spattering

This final touch can be done before the design is painted, or when it is finished. I prefer the latter. Cover the design area before spattering. Thin the paint with turpentine and load an old flat brush, then run your thumbnail over the bristles. Test your paint over scrap paper first. If the paint is too thin the specking will bleed; if it isn't thin enough, it won't come out of the brush.

Preparing Porcelain and Glass

Porcelain should be lightly sprayed with Krylon Matte #1311 before the pattern is applied. If it is rough, sand it with very fine sandpaper. To prepare glass for reverse painting, it must be cleaned well with ammonia or an ammonia-based cleaner. Once clean, don't allow your fingers to touch the surface while inking the pattern on the glass. Once the inking is done, spray the glass with Illinois Bronze Clear Plastic or Krylon Matte #1311. The Krylon spray gives the glass a frosted finish, but once placed on the backing, the glass ap-

pears clear. For clear glass, clean as described and then spray it with Illinois Bronze Clear Plastic or undercoat the design area with Winsor & Newton's Liquin and allow it to dry a few minutes before applying the paint.

Frosting Glass

Wash and dry the glass very well. Apply an etching compound to the glass with a palette knife. Take the frosting tool (a round steel piece with a handle) and work with moderate pressure in a circular motion, covering the entire top surface. Rinse with water and dry. Repeat this procedure until all areas are evenly etched. Paint on the frosted side of the glass. It isn't necessary to put a finish over the completed painting. To clean the painted piece, wash with soap and water.

Applying Gold or Silver Leaf

Sand and seal as described in the Preparing Wood section. The surface should be very smooth. Traditionally the surface is painted with Red Iron Oxide for gold leafing and Black or Red Iron Oxide for silver leafing, although any base color may be used. Cover your work area with wax paper. Brush the sizing (glue) on the area you want to leaf. When the sizing has turned clear and is tacky to the touch, it is ready for the leaf to be applied. Cut each sheet of leafing in half or smaller. This makes it easier to handle and reduces waste. Place the leaf on the sizing until all glue is covered. Brush over the leaf with a very soft bristle brush to be certain it is pushed into the sizing. With a cotton ball or large, soft brush, softly brush away excess edges of leafing outside the sized area. Let the leafing dry for twenty-four hours and then buff with a cotton ball or piece of velvet. Seal the leaf with Krylon Crystal Clear. You may then antique it if desired. Varnish with several light coats to protect the leaf from tarnishing.

Preparing Tin

Wash the piece in vinegar water and then in soap and water. Dry well. Seal the tin with a flat, rustproof spray paint. Use this as your basecoat, or spray it with an acrylic color.

Finishing

After the painting is dry, carefully remove any graphite lines with an eraser or with soap and water. Wipe with a tack cloth. Using Krylon Satin Finish Varnish or Blair Satin Varnish, apply several very light coats, following the directions on the can. Wet-sand between the last few coats. The sandpaper can be dipped in hot, soapy water—the soap acts as a cushion between the surface and the sandpaper. After the varnish has dried for several days, apply a very thin, even coat of parquet wax (such as Winsor & Newton's Wax Varnish), using #0000 steel wool. Allow to dry for a few minutes and buff to a beautiful sheen with a soft cloth.

In place of spray varnish you may also use a waterbase varnish such as Right Step—be sure the varnish you choose is recommended for use over oils.

Tips for Successful Painting

Transferring the Design

An important first step to decorative painting is the tracing and transferring of your designs. Use care in tracing the pattern and be as exact as you can. Many problems can be avoided if you start with a good tracing. Always trace with a felt-tip pen. Position the tracing on the painting surface so it is located correctly and secure with masking tape. Slide a graphite sheet under the tracing. Use a stylus to obtain crisp, clear lines, but don't press hard as you will make indentations in the wood.

Loading Your Brush and Brush Mixing

In the following projects, a **plus sign** (+) means to brush mix the colors listed together. Don't overload the paint on the brush as you're mixing (you don't have to mix all the color for the area at one time). Variation in the mixture will add interest to your painting. When loading the brush, pull the paint from the edge of the puddle with pressure, then go to the next color and mix them together. If you load and brush mix in this manner, the chances of getting too much paint will be significantly reduced. The order of the colors in the color set-up indicates the amount of each color used: use more of the first color, less of the second color, etc.

Loading your brush correctly is so important. Never pick up your paint off the top of the puddle. If you do, I guarantee you will have it gunked on your brush up to the farrel. This will put too much paint on the surface and will destroy the brush much faster than necessary. The correct way to load your brush is to pull the paint out with pressure (the farrel of the brush should almost touch the palette pad). If brush-mixing, pull the second color out in the same way and pressure the colors together until you have the proper value. If more than two colors are required, pick the additional colors up in the same way. Always leave your palette paper on the pad so you can apply pressure without having to hold the palette pad. Brush-mixing creates variation in your mixtures, which will add interest and sparkle to your painting.

Using the Right Amount of Pressure When Blending

Always apply the paint with pressure. Turn your work so that when you need a sharp edge, the chisel edge of the brush is placed next to the line. To blend successfully, dry wipe your brush before beginning, place it half on the highlight or shading color and half on the base color, then pull with pressure using short, crosshatching strokes, working one color into the other to remove the outside perimeter line. Dry wipe often if needed. If the highlight or shading color is moving, load a very small amount of the base color on your brush to help control this color.

Once the outside edge of an area is blended, dry wipe the brush and lightly whisper it over the remaining area, just barely softening the color. If this step is overdone, the highlight or shading color may have to be strengthened again. To recap, when applying paint or removing hard, definite lines, do so with pressure. Use very little pressure on the brush when something needs to be softened or just barely needs touching up. Using the right amount of pressure is important to becoming a good painter.

If you're having problems blending your paint, you're probably applying too much paint in the original application. As you add darks and highlights, they will slip and slide if too much paint was applied, particularly if it was not applied with pressure in the original application. In fact, if using oils, the first application of paint should be light enough that the background color shows through. Note the scant amount of paint in the step-by-step application on page 10 when using color side by side, and how rough and choppy the colors are applied at the beginning of the blending process. If using more alkyds than oils, use more paint.

Dry Wiping

A **dash** (—) in the following projects means to dry wipe your brush and proceed to the next color. Never clean your brush with turpentine when you're going from one color to the next. Simply dry wipe and neutralize your brush by loading it with Yellow Ochre or white and then dry wiping it several times.

Buff Areas

Often in the **buff** area (think of this area as the buffer zone between the dark and light values), you may have more than one color listed. You may wish to use only one of these colors. At other times all the buffing colors are required (such as on a large object or one where you are using colors that will become muddy if mixed directly, and therefore need several buffing colors to keep the darks from the lights). If the instructions call for the same color setup for all the objects of one type (such as all the grapes, or all the leaves) these different buffing colors will help you get the variations needed to make these objects different.

Optional Colors

A color in **parentheses** means this color is optional. If you use it, do so sparingly. Optional colors give you a way to add variation to all the objects painted with the same colors.

Dark Areas

These are the darkest inked areas on the design and represent shadows and areas overlapped by other objects.

Light Areas

These areas are applied last. As they are applied, they are pulled into the buffing color or dark areas with short, choppy strokes—thus beginning the blending process. This is an example of using color side by side, which results in more contrast (see left illustration on page 10).

When a light, soft color or very dark value is desired, it is easier to obtain this by blocking in the entire object with a light or dark value. The dark areas are deepened with shading and the light areas are lightened with highlights. This is using color on top of color (see illustration at right).

Shading

Shading means to darken the deeper triangles and overlapped areas in the dark areas (not the entire dark area). Apply with pressure and only blend the edge of the color that needs to be softened. Do not make the dark area all the same value—keep one portion of the dark area several values darker.

Highlights

Highlights are used to strengthen the light areas and to add sparkle. These are built up in layers. Each time they are added, the area is smaller and the value is lighter. This is called *stacking the highlights*. Apply the highlights with pressure and blend only the outside edge first, then soften very lightly over the entire highlight area.

Tints and Accent Colors

Accent colors are usually placed in the midvalue area, or applied from the outside edge. An accent color is pure color from the tube. A tint is color mixed with white. A tint can be applied in the same area as an accent color. Add these when most of the elements in the design have been painted, so that each one is related and the flow of color is controlled.

Glazing

A glaze is a thin film of color laid over a dry underpainting. A painting can be glazed as many times as you like—each time you achieve more depth, more true color and sparkle. To glaze, load a clean brush with Winsor & Newton's Blending and Glazing Medium, blot it on a paper towel and lightly skim the medium over the area to be worked. Load your brush with very little paint. Transparent colors work best, as the color underneath is supposed to glimmer through, but opaque colors can become transparent when applied over the blending medium. The glazing medium usually stays workable for thirty minutes or longer. If it feels like the paint isn't moving, let it dry and apply the glazing mixture again.

Scumbling

Scumbling color over a dried underpainting will achieve almost the same effect, but with a rougher texture. The high shines can also be achieved by scumbling. The key to success is to use very little paint. If you don't like what you have done or the colors have become muddy, you can remove the paint with a piece of paper towel. Learning to scumble or glaze may be easiest if you work on one area at a time, allowing it to dry before you move on to the next area.

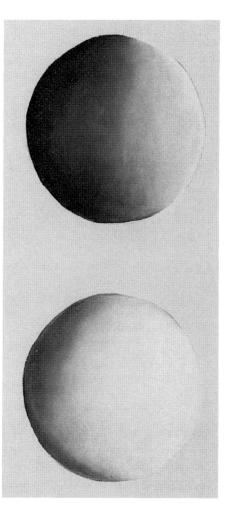

◀ Color Side by Side

With this technique, you block the color in side by side, creating a strong contrast within your subject. Using color in this manner will create a color gradation (a dark, middle and light value) in the object when you blend. Notice the rough, choppy edge of each of the colors in the block-in. Begin the blending by placing the brush half on both colors and pulling one into the other with pressure and short, choppy strokes. When all the hard, definite lines are broken between the colors, reduce the pressure on the brush and begin to refine. This requires a soft touch, which will take practice to develop. The key to blending is knowing when to use pressure and when to whisper over your paint.

Color on Top of Color ▶

In this technique the entire object is blocked in with one color, allowing you to create an object with less contrast. This may be a very light object or a very dark one. The circle in the illustration is blocked in with white and the black is placed on top of this. You will begin the blending by placing your brush half on the dark and half on the base color. Break the line between the dark and light areas with pressure, then lighten the pressure as the dark is blended out over the light area. Learn to recognize when to use pressure and when to use a very light touch.

Understanding the Basic Elements of Painting

These six elements are present in every painting. We will touch lightly on all of these, but will deal with several of them in greater depth.

Motivation is the reason for the painting. Without this, the other elements or principles would be similar to a band without a conductor. One must be motivated before one paints.

Composition is the design the subject imposes on the surface and the balance in opposites of shapes, colors and values that make the painting a whole.

Drawing is the result of three elements: perspective, proportion and anatomy. All of these together result in correct and realistic shapes. Drawing ability can be acquired if practiced diligently. I learned to draw from tracing patterns.

Value creates a three-dimensional effect on a flat surface and is one of the properties of color. If a painting appears flat, it is lacking value change. There should be only one source of strong light, just as in nature there is only one source of light, the sun. Light only travels in a straight line. A three-dimensional painting has at least three values: light, medium and dark. Within these values there should be several more values. The more value change an object has, the more dimension it takes on.

Body tone or middle value is the area of the object that is being illuminated. The shapes in a design will vary in values because of their individual texture, color and placement within the design. Middle value is also the value we often lose. The middle-value area is where tints and accents are often added.

Shadow areas appear on a three-dimensional shape because the straight rays of light cannot hit all of its areas. The shadow area is the portion of the shape receding from the light.

Reflected light or dull light is caused by light bouncing off a nearby surface or another object into the shadowed side. Reflected light is never lighter than the body tone and is also cooler in temperature.

Highlights appear on the shape directly in line with the main source of light. They appear where a concave or convex shape is facing the light. The color is often obscured because of the glaring illumination, but the highlight can be absent because of a dull, nonreflective surface.

Lost-and-found edges describe the outer edges of an object. A lost edge is fuzzy and indistinct and appears where shapes recede into the background or into an adjacent object of the same value. A found edge is sharply defined and comes forward. Lost-and-found edges help to create the illusion of depth.

Rhythm is the repetition of a texture created with a brush technique. Each item has its own special textures and must be painted so its characteristics can be differentiated from the other objects.

Color

Unlike the previous six elements, color is not present in all art forms—such as pen-and-ink drawings and graphite sketches—nonetheless, it is a very important element. But remember, paintings are not built with color alone. Color must be coordinated with value, drawing, composition, motivation, lost-and-found edges and rhythm.

The primary colors are red, yellow and blue. Primary colors cannot be made by mixing any other colors—they are pure pigments. When you mix two primaries, a secondary color is formed: orange, green and violet. This gives us six basic colors.

A color's complement is found opposite it on the color wheel. The complementary colors are red and green, yellow and violet, and blue and orange. A color wheel can be a great help in choosing color schemes and mixing colors.

Color has three characteristics: hue, value and intensity. *Hue* is the name of the color's family. For instance, there is a yellow-green family and a blue-green family. You must classify manufactured colors into the proper color family in order to use them correctly for mixing and neutralizing. (A color can be neutralized, or toned down, by mixing it with its complement or an earth-tone color.)

A color in its normal state is thought to be either warm or cool. Warm colors will cause a subject to advance; cool colors will recede. The complement of a warm color is always cool. A warm color may appear cooler when placed next to a warmer color—color is relative.

Value is the degree of lightness or darkness of a color. Each color can range in tone anywhere between almost white to almost black. Value is the most important of the characteristics of color because it creates form. An object will appear larger if painted a light value than if the same object were painted a dark value. Value creates emphasis and space. Strong values contrast and demand attention to pull the eye to the foreground. Closely related values tend to recede and minimize. A light value will appear lighter when placed next to a very dark value, and the reverse applies to dark values.

Intensity is the strength, purity or brightness of a color. A color straight from the tube is at its most intense; a color mixed with white or neutralized can become dull. Don't confuse intensity and value: A dark-value color can still be bright or high in intensity (such as Dioxazine Purple straight from the tube), and a light-value color can be dull (such as a light pink grayed down to produce a dusky rose color). Intense, pure colors pull attention to themselves, and create a vibration in the painting. Remember all of these keys!

Golden Apple Step by Step

On this project you will be using color side by side (see left illustration on page 10) to develop a round object with an upper right light source. For these conditions, I divide the object into fourths. The highlight will be in the upper right quadrant and the strongest dark in the lower left quadrant. The dull light will not go past six o'clock or ten o'clock.

1 Load your brush with RS first, then move to YO and mix the two colors on your palette. Apply the color with short, choppy strokes in the shadow area. This crescent area must go at least half to two-thirds of the way around the apple. The dark area color is placed in the stem hole also. Only the stem hole should have a hard, definite edge. Dry wipe your brush and load it with a mixture of YO + NY. Place this buffing mixture around the entire dark shadow area, creating a middle value. The blending process begins as you apply this buffing color and pull it into the dark area. Dry wipe and pressure load your brush with NYH + CL. Block in the remainder of the apple. Apply the block-in colors with pressure, using very little paint and allowing some of the background to peek through if painting with oils. If using alkyds, the coverage should be heavier, completely covering the background.

2 You began the blending process as you applied the colors on the apple, but more blending is required once all the colors are blocked in. Using less pressure on the brush, work between the colors, pulling one into the other with short, choppy strokes. When blending the lower shadow area, turn the apple and blend across its width. Be careful the light area remains in the upper right quadrant. Dry wipe often while you are blending. If you've applied too much paint, lay a tissue down flat on the apple and blot the excess. Load your brush with DP + RS (the yellow's value is lowered by mixing it with its complementary color, violet). If you can't get the crescent as dark as you would like, pick up the same mixture with a touch of Blk. Apply the shading colors with pressure in the lower half of the shadow area and in the stem hole. Dry wipe your brush. With less pressure, blend between the colors, removing any hard, definite lines. The darkest area of the crescent can touch the outside edge of the apple in the lower shadow area.

3 Dry wipe your brush. With pressure, apply the first highlight mixture of W + CL in a choppy fashion. Consider which area of the apple is protruding the most and make the highlight larger in that direction. Dry wipe and apply a lighter value of W + CL in a smaller area on top of the first highlight. Dry wipe and load the brush with W. Apply this color with pressure in a smaller area on top of the two previous highlights. This is called *stacking the highlights*.

4 With less pressure on the brush, use short, choppy strokes to work the outside edge of the highlight. Work across the apple as well as up and down to prevent the highlight from spreading to the bottom of the apple. Once the outside edge of the highlight has been softened, lightly whisper the brush over the entire highlight to soften it. Refine the apple by lightly blending along the contour. Check to see you have at least three values in the apple. Apply a light green tint in the middle value area with CGP. Use pressure to apply the tint, then lightly blend. Add a touch of CYD and blend out. Add a cool gray (W + Blk) with pressure to the outside edge for a dull reflected light, making it wider in one area. Place the brush half on the reflected light and half on the base color of the apple, then blend with short, choppy or crisscross strokes. The resting area right under the apple is BU + Blk. Pull the color out with your brush and work shades of yellow and W + Blk into the outside edges. The resting area must be parallel to the bottom edge of the surface and very thin right in front of the apple.

Golden Apple Step by Step

Teacher's Apple

Pattern and instructions for Teacher's Apple *on page 14.*

Teacher's Apple

I hope you will enjoy painting this design. This apple looks really nice on a plate with a schoolhouse design, making a perfect gift for a favorite teacher.

Surface Preparation

Sand and seal the plate with Designs From the Heart Wood Sealer. Stain with a very light wash of BU. Deepen the edges and around the schoolhouses with BU + Blk.

Apple

Dark area	RS + YO
Buff	YO + NYH
Light area	NYH + CL
Shade	DP + RS + (Blk)
Highlight	W + CL − W
Tint	CGP
	W + Blk
Accent	CYD

Leaf and Stem

Dark area	Blk + CL + W
Buff	YO
Light area	Dark area mix + CL + W
Shade	Dark area mix + Blk
Tint	W + Blk

Source

The schoolhouse plate may be ordered from
A Touch of Class by Aileen
11215 Inverness Ct. NE
Albuquerque, NM 87111-7547

Green Apples and Blossoms

Green Apples and Blossoms

Top
left

Surface Preparation

Sand and seal the shelf with Designs From the Heart Wood Sealer. Paint the shelf with a light wash of Ceramcoat Light Ivory. Paint the edges with Ceramcoat Village Green. Antique the edges and spatter the surface with the mixture for the light green apple: PG + CGP + CL + Blk + W.

 ### Source

The apple shelf may be ordered from
A Touch of Class by Aileen
11215 Inverness Ct. NE
Albuquerque, NM 87111-7547

Light-Value Apple

Base	CGP + YO
Shade	PG + RS + (Blk)
Highlight	CGP + W − W
Tint	W + Blk
Accent	CYD

Dark-Value Apple

Dark area	PG + RS + (Blk)
Buff	YO − CYD
Light area	CGP + YO + (CL + W)
Shade	PG + RS + Blk
Highlight	CGP + W − W
Tint	W + Blk

Blossoms

Base	NYL + W
Shade	PG + CGP + RS
Highlight	W + CL − W
Tint	RS

Blossom Centers

Base	YO
Shade	PG + Blk + RS
Highlight	W + CL − W
Lines	Blk + RS
Dark splotches	Blk + RS
Light splotches	W + CL

Light-Value Leaves

Base	PG + CL + W
Shade	PG + RS + (Blk)
Highlight	CGP + W − W
Tint	RS

Middle- and Dark-Value Leaves

Dark area	PG + CL + (Blk)
Buff	RS
Light area	Dark area mix + CL + W
Shade	Dark area mix + Blk
Highlight	W + CL − W
Tint	W + Blk

Branch

Dark area	Blk + RS
Light area	CL + W
Shade	Dark area mix + Blk
Highlight	W + CL − W

Bottom right

More Apples

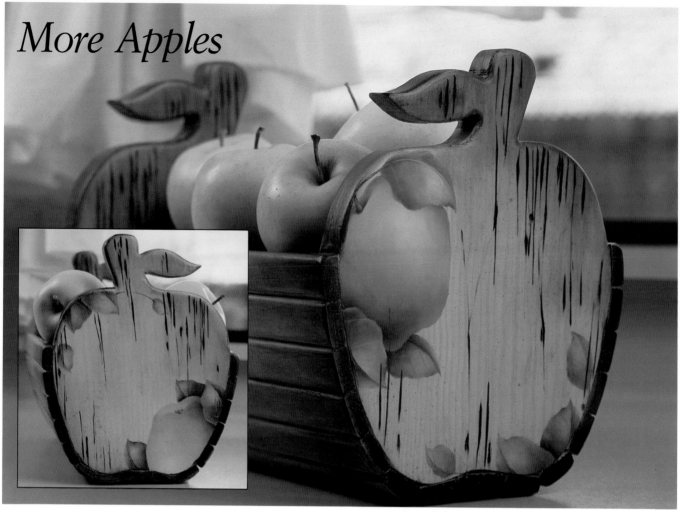

Surface Preparation

Sand and seal the basket with Designs From the Heart Wood Sealer. Paint the entire basket with Ceramcoat Ivory. Antique with BU. After the design is painted, deepen the edges and sides with BU + Blk. I distressed the basket with an ice pick, but do be careful! Work away from yourself and keep the distressing very irregular.

Source

This adorable basket may be ordered from
A Touch of Class by Aileen
11215 Inverness Ct. NE
Albuquerque, NM 87111-7547

Golden Apples

Dark area	YO + RS
Buff	YO + NYH
Light area	CL + NYH
Shade	RS + DP + (Blk)
Highlight	W + CL − W
Tint	W + Blk
Accent	CGP

Leaves

Dark area	Blk + CL + W
Buff	YO − RS
Light area	Dark area mix + CL + W
Shade	Dark area mix + Blk − Dark area mix + Blk + RS + DP
Highlight	W + CL − W
Tint	W + Blk

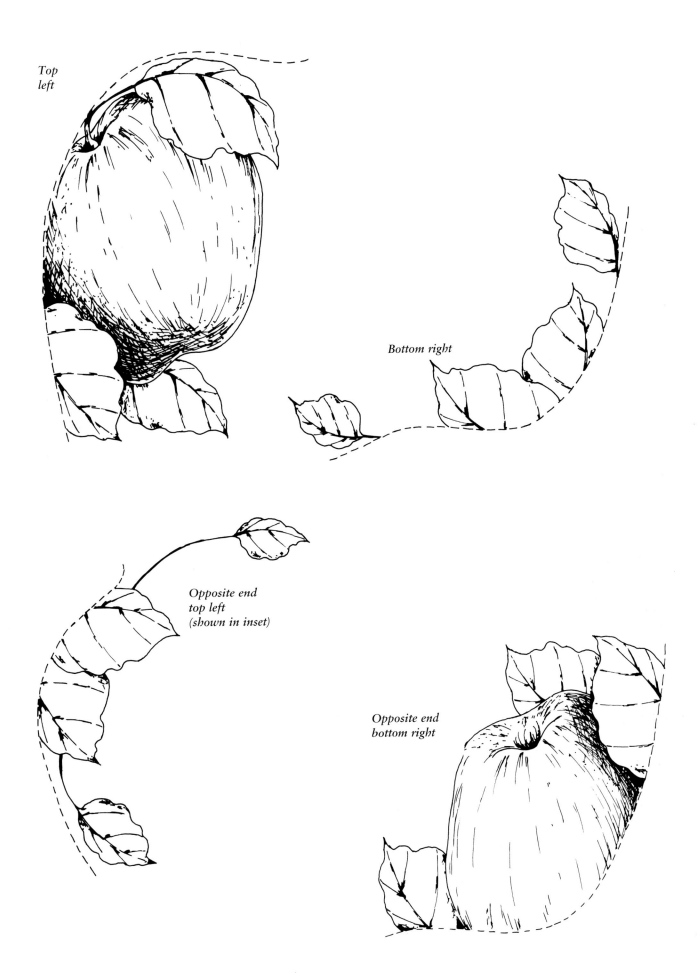

Top
left

Bottom right

Opposite end
top left
(shown in inset)

Opposite end
bottom right

Blossom Step by Step

Create this blossom using color on top of color (see right illustration on page 10). If you prefer to apply your colors side by side, block in the dark area first on all the petals, then the buffing color or colors, and then the light area colors. Blend the colors, then shade and highlight. The color setup for the yellow blossom uses its complementary color for shading.

1 Block in all the petals and flips with CL + NYL. Leave a small space separating the petals and flips so you won't lose your pattern. Load a no. 2 flat brush with RS + Blk + DP. Pressure this color in the areas as shown on the illustration above. When placing shading underneath a petal, make it heavier in the darker shadow areas and lighter in the areas where the petals overlap less.

2 Blend between the colors with soft, choppy strokes, working across the width of the petal. Don't overblend. If you don't see at least two dark values in the shadow areas, go back and deepen the triangular-shaped shadow areas again.

3 Highlight the petals with W + CL and then W. Stack the highlights (see page 10) on the petals, applying pressure. Don't build all the highlights to a pure white. Some should be built with W + CL and then W, and some with W + CL only.

Flips

To achieve the feeling that the flip is turned, there must be a second-value dark on the surface at both ends of the flip. Take the chisel edge of the brush and pull the light from the flip to connect to the petal. See page 52 for step-by-step instructions on creating flips.

Center

1 Block in the center with YO, making it irregular in shape.

2 Add a crescent-shaped shadow using RS + DP. Blend the edge of the crescent with short pressure strokes.

3 Pressure the highlight into the center with W + CL, and then W. Blend only the edge of the highlight with short pressure strokes. Sometimes I use both lines and splotches on a center, but I chose to use only the splotches on this blossom. Flatten the tip of your liner brush with pressure so you have splotches, not dots. Apply RS + DP, then CL + W with pressure. Make some of the splotches large and some small. Splotches should fall out on the petal, but don't create an even ring around the center.

A Yellow Blossom

Surface Preparation

Refer to the glass frosting techniques on page 8. Frosted glass is a delight to paint on. If your oils bleed out in a ring around the design area, wash the painting in ammonia when the design is dry. If this doesn't remove the ring, mask the clear glass edges with masking tape and lightly spray with Krylon Matte #1311.

Blossom

Base	CL + NYL
Shade	RS + Blk + (DP)
Highlight	W + CL − W

Blossom Center

Base	YO
Shade	RS + DP
Highlight	W + CL − W
Splotches	RS + DP
	CL + W

Leaves

Dark area	Blk + CL + W
Buff	YO − RS
Light area	Dark area mix + CL + W
Shade	Dark area mix + Blk + (PB)
Highlight	W + CL − W
Tint	W + Blk

 ### Source

The glass box, glass frosting compound and tool may be ordered from A Touch of Class by Aileen
11215 Inverness Ct. NE
Albuquerque, NM 87111-7547

Ribbon Step by Step

Color Side by Side

1 Block in the dark area (where the ribbon is tucked under another ribbon or knot, or turns or bends). Leave the outer edge rough and hacky. Load the brush with the buffing color and apply adjacent to all the dark areas. Blend the two colors together by working across the ribbon. Block in the remainder of the ribbon with the light area mix. Blend into the buffing color by blending the colors together across the width of the ribbon.

2 Load the brush with the shading color, apply with pressure in all the dark areas, not allowing the shading outside of the original dark area. Edge-blend the edge of the shading into the dark area. If this shading is not dark enough, deepen with a value one shade deeper in the deeper triangle areas.

3 Load the brush with the highlight color and stack the highlights, letting each one get smaller in size but lighter in value. The highlight should be the full width of the ribbon in the fat, full areas of the ribbon. When the highlights are all applied, dry wipe the brush and edge-blend the outside edge of the first highlight by blending across the width of the ribbon. Soften the outside edge of the second highlight and then the last highlight. Dry wipe the brush and gently soften over the entire ribbon, pulling with the length of the ribbon. Highlight only the parts of the ribbon coming towards you or being lifted up. The ribbon needs a small highlight on the rolled edge, which may be done with a small flat or a liner brush.

4 Use the tint (W + Blk) as a highlight on the ribbon going away from you or receding into the background. It may be stacked with a touch of pure W on top of the tint. These tints are blended as described above for the highlights. Another tint might be added to carry color through the design and these are edge-blended and then lightly softened over by pulling or blending the length of the ribbon.

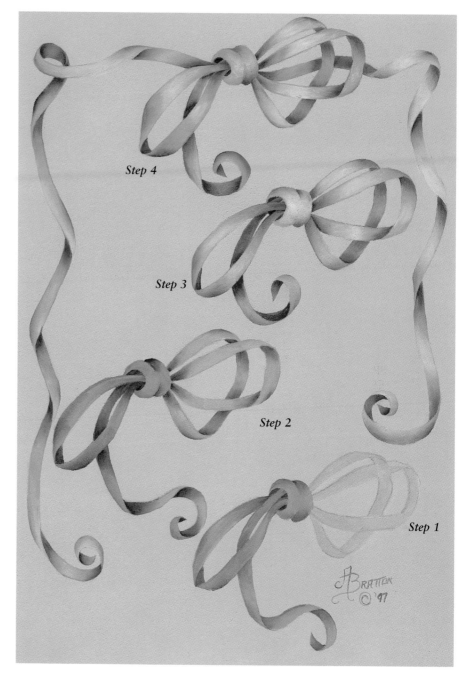

Step 4

Step 3

Step 2

Step 1

Color on Top of Color

1 Block in the entire ribbon with the base color, trying to cover the graphite lines.

2 Shade as described in step 2 of Color Side by Side.

3 Highlight as described in step 3 of Color Side by Side.

4 Tint with the W + Blk as described in step 4 of Color Side by Side. A middle value may be added with a tint that carries the color through the design.

Victorian Blossoms

Victorian Blossoms

This little musical trunk looked like it needed to be decorated with beautiful Victorian blossoms. I lined the inside with ecru taffeta, then painted a blossom and leaves in one corner. Paint on the taffeta with your oils or alkyds just as on any other surface.

Surface Preparation

Sand, seal and paint with several coats of Americana Dusty Rose. Wet sand between coats if necessary. Mist lightly with Krylon Matte #1311. Apply pattern with graphite very lightly.

Source

This trunk may be ordered from A Touch of Class by Aileen 11215 Inverness Ct. NE Albuquerque, NM 87111-7547

Light-Value Blossom

Base	NYL + NYR
Shade	DP + AC + NYH + (Blk)
Highlight	NYL + W − W
Tint	CL + W

Middle-Value Blossom

Dark area	DP + AC + NYH
Light area	NYL + NYR
Shade	DP + AC + NYH + Blk
Highlight	NYL + W − W
Tint	W + Blk

Dark-Value Blossom

Base	DP + AC + NYH
Shade	Base + Blk
Highlight	NYH − NYL + NYR
Tint	W + Blk

Blossom Centers

Base	NYH
Shade	DP + AC + NYH
Highlight	CL + W − W
Lines	DP + AC + NYH + Blk
Dots	DP + AC + NYH + Blk
	W + Blk

Leaves

Dark area	Blk + CL + (W)
Buff	YO
Light area	Dark area mix + CL + W
Shade	Dark area mix + Blk
	Dark area mix + Blk + (PB)
Highlight	W + CL − W
Tint	W + Blk

Accent Leaves

Dark area	DP + RS
Buff	CGP
Light area	CGP + CL + W
Shade	DP + RS + Blk
Highlight	W + CL − W
Tint	W + Blk

Ribbon

Base	NYR
Shade	DP + AC + NYH + (Blk)
Highlight	NYL + W − W

Berries

Base	DP + AC + NYH + (Blk)
Shade	Base + Blk
Highlight	NYR + NYL − NYL

More Blossoms

Surface Preparation

Sand, seal and put a light wash of Ceramcoat Ivory on the top surface. Paint the drawers with Americana Medium Flesh plus a touch of Ceramcoat Ivory. Lightly antique the corners of the top with BU. Gold leaf all the edges and knobs on the drawers (refer to page 8 for gold leafing instructions). To complete the project, lightly spatter the drawers and top with BU.

 Source

You may order this jewelry box from
A Touch of Class by Aileen
11215 Inverness Ct. NE
Albuquerque, NM 87111-7547

More Blossoms *instructions continued on page 28.*

More Blossoms

Continued from page 27.

Light-Value Blossom

Base	NYL
Shade	AC + CRL + RS − AC + CRL + RS + Blk
Highlight	W + CL − W
Tint	W + Blk

Middle-Value Blossom

Dark area	AC + RS + CRL
Buff	CRL + YO − CYD
Light area	Buff + NYL
Shade	AC + RS + Blk
Highlight	NY + NYL − NYL + W
Tint	W + Blk

Dark-Value Blossom

Base	AC + CRL + RS + (CYD)
Shade	Base mix + Blk
Highlight	NYH + NYL − NYL + W
Tint	W + Blk

Tiny Blossoms
Use all of the above colors.

Light-Value Leaves

Base	PG + CL + W
Shade	Base mix + Blk
Highlight	W
Tint	W + Blk
Accent	AC + CRL + RS

Middle and Dark Value Leaves

Dark area	PG + CL + W + (Blk)
Buff	YO − RS
Light area	Dark area mix + CL + W
Shade	Dark area mix + Blk
Highlight	W + CL − W
Tint	W + Blk
Accent	AC + CRL + RS

Accent Leaves

Dark area	AC + RS + Blk
Buff	PG + CL + W + (Blk) + CGP
Light area	Buff mix + CL + W
Shade	AC + RS + Blk − Blk
Highlight	W + CL − W
Tint	W + Blk

Daisy Step by Step

1

2

First Stroke

Second Stroke

3

4

Third Stroke

Daisy Step by Step

This is a flat-brush-blended daisy, which allows you to blend and shape the petals. Consider the position and perspective of the daisy when tracing the pattern. If you're looking straight into the daisy, the petals will all be the same length and the scooped-out area in the flower's center will be perfectly centered. If you're looking at the daisy from an angle, as in the illustration on the previous page, the petals in the front are longer and the scooped-out area in the center will be very close to the back edge of the daisy. Also, you will be unable to see where the back petals connect to the center.

1 Place a mixture of Blk + RS at the base of each petal (where the petal goes into the center), stretching the paint lengthwise about one-half to two-thirds of the way down the petal. Keep the mixture heavier and darker at the base. Place dark values where a petal is under another petal so you're building shape and dimension.

2 Buff sideways across the bottom of the dark area with YO. Only two-thirds of the petal should be blocked in at this stage.

3 Begin the overstroking with your no. 6 flat brush loaded with W + (CL). Every white flower has yellow in it—if you start with pure white, you can't build a lighter highlight. If you're painting on a blue background, use a touch of YO instead of the CL because CL will give you a green tint. Work underneath petals first. The shape of the petals should vary: A few crisp, sharp edges portray a feeling of freshness, while too many round edges give a wilted feeling. The first overstroke begins to shape the bottom and the right edge of the petal. The second overstroke will finish shaping the bottom and the left edge of the petal. The third overstroke is the center stroke, and pulls up into the petal (but not very far). Don't destroy the dark area that was applied first. To soften the area between the last stroke and the dark area, blend across the width of the petal.

4 The petal tip is usually done with pure white, but you can add tints of color on some of the petals at this time. The petals that fall in the lightest area should be lighter in value— this area should correspond to where the light is hitting the center. If need be, build stronger highlights and dark shadow areas on some of the petals when the daisy is dry.

The Center

1 Block in the entire center with YO, being certain you pull the color down around the petals on the front edge of the center to make them appear to grow out of the center. (You could also paint the center first and then pull the petals into it.)

2 Study how light hits the opening of a round container to accurately paint the scooped-out area of the flower's center. The strongest light hits on the outside of the scooped-out area, and the strongest dark is on the inside. Opposite the strong dark inside is a dull light. On the outside of the dull light is a dull dark. Using the handle of the brush or stylus, pull out paint to form the scooped-out area. With a no. 2 flat brush, place RS + Blk with pressure inside the circle in the dark area. Apply the remaining paint left in the brush outside the circle. Blend the darks in by placing the brush half on the dark and half on the base color of the center. Soften with short, choppy strokes.

3 Apply the highlights by stacking them with pressure (see page 10) using a no. 2 flat brush. The first highlight is CYD placed in the strong light area outside the circle. Without reloading the brush, apply this color to the dull light area inside the circle. Apply CL + W and then W over the highlight and dull reflected area. Blend the bottom edge of these highlights. If they aren't strong enough, reapply them. Apply a dull, reflected light (tint) of W + Blk to the outside edge of the center, below the dull dark on the back outside edge of the scooped-out area.

4 The "splotches" are applied with Blk, using the corner of your no. 4 flat brush. Vary the size and distance from center so they don't create an even ring. The splotches on a daisy viewed from an angle will only appear along the front edge of the center and out on the petals all around. You will not be able to see the splotches on the back edge of the center.

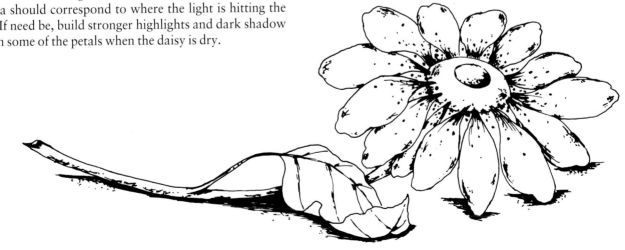

Daisy in the Round

Surface Preparation

The rim of the round plate with the inked border of leaves is Ceramcoat Light Ivory. The center and edge is Creamcoat Village Green. Antique the inside edge of the center area and the edge of the plate with a mixture of Blk + CL + W, then spatter them very lightly with the same mixture. See Tips for Inking on page 37 to create the ring of leaves on the outer rim of the plate. The inking should be done before you spray the surface with Krylon Matte #1311, as the ink won't adhere once the surface has been sprayed.

Daisy

Dark area	RS + Blk
Buff	YO
Overstroke	W + (CL) − W

Center

Base	YO
Shade	RS + Blk
Highlight	CYD − CL + W − W
Tint	W + Blk
Splotches	Blk

Light- and Middle-Value Leaves

Dark area	Blk + CL + W
Buff	YO − RS
Light area	Dark area mix + CL + W
Shade	Dark area mix + Blk
Highlight	W + CL − W
Tint	W + Blk

Dark-Value Leaves

Dark area	Blk + OC + CL
Buff	RS
Light area	Dark area mix + CL + W
Shade	Dark area mix + Blk + (PB)
Highlight	W + CL − W
Tint	W + Blk

Source

The wooden plate may be ordered from
A Touch of Class by Aileen
11215 Inverness Ct. NE
Albuquerque, NM 87111-7547

Daisy in the Round

Daisies and Violets
From the Heart

I couldn't resist painting on this beautiful glass heart. The clear bevel in the center would look really lovely with an initial etched on it.

Surface Preparation

Mask off the clear glass bevel with tape and paper. Spray the blue glass with Krylon Matte #1311 as this will make the glass easier to paint on. Refer to the photo opposite for placement of the tendrils. Paint the violets as shown on page 35. Use the color setup given on page 30 to paint the center of the daisies and leaves.

Daisies

Dark area	RS + Blk + (PB)
Buff	YO
Overstroke	W + YO − W
Tint	W + PB + Blk

Source

This glass heart can be ordered from
A Touch of Class by Aileen
11215 Inverness Ct. NE
Albuquerque, NM 87111-7547

Violets on a Box

Surface Preparation
Spray the box lightly with Krylon Matte #1311 before the pattern is applied.

Light-Value Violet

Base	PB + Blk + AC + W
Shade	PB + Blk
Highlight	W
Tint	AC + W − W + Blk

Middle-Value Violet

Dark area	PB + Blk + AC
Light area	Dark area mix + W
Shade	Dark area mix + PB + Blk
Highlight	W
Accent	AC

Dark-Value Violet

Base	PB + Blk + AC + DP
Highlight	W
Tint	W + Blk − AC

Violet Center

Upside down V	PB + Blk
Center dot	CRL
Splotches	W + CL

Leaves

Dark area	Blk + CL + W
Buff	YO
Light area	Dark area mix + CL + W + (CGP)
Shade	Dark area mix + Blk + (PB)
Highlight	W + CL − W

Finished project shown on page 32.

Violet Step by Step

To paint the light- and dark-value violets, use color on top of color, as shown on page 10. For the middle-value violets, use color side by side. The instructions below are for a light- or dark-value violet.

1 Block in the violet with a light-value mix or a dark value. On the light value, use pressure to place the shading color (PB + Blk) with a no. 2 flat brush as illustrated. If you are painting a dark-value violet, it will not be necessary to shade.

2 Place the highlights on the petals as shown in the illustration. Stack the highlights with pressure, using a no. 4 flat brush (see page 10). Stack the highlights on the big, full center petal and at least one of the top petals. Blend with short, choppy strokes and, if necessary, strengthen the highlights again.

3 Establish stronger tints (if desired) and add the center. Using the liner brush, paint the upside down V-shape with a mixture of PB + Blk mixed with a blending medium. Place a dot of CRL in the crook of the upside down V, and place a few W + CL splotches inside and outside the open end of the V.

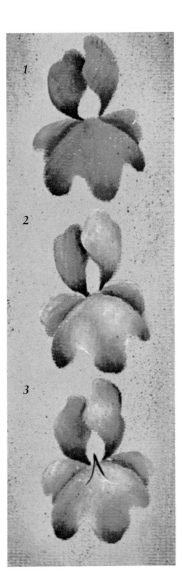

Pattern for puffed heart, page 37.

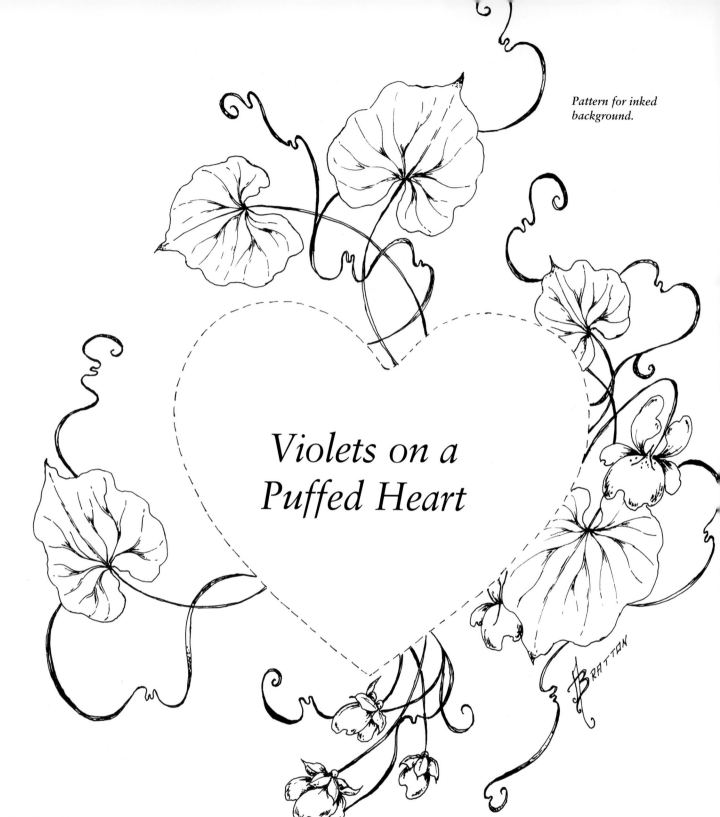

Pattern for inked background.

Violets on a Puffed Heart

BRATTON

Surface Preparation

Sand and seal the puffed heart and frame with Designs From the Heart Wood Sealer. Paint the puffed heart with Ceramcoat Lavendar Lace. Paint the frame with a lighter mixture of three parts Lavendar Lace and one part Ceramcoat Ivory. Spatter the frame softly with PB + Blk + W. Paint the masonite background of the frame with Ceramcoat Ivory. Ink the design on the background, following the tips on the next page. When the ink has dried for at least six hours, spray the inking with Krylon Matte #1311. Pick up Blending and Glazing Medium on your brush, then load it with the leaf colors. This will make the paint very thin. Apply a light tint of color to the dark areas of the inked design, then buff out the highlights with a tissue. Tint the inked violets with the violet colors in the same way. Lace was added under the heart before gluing the heart to the frame.

Tips for Inking

I prefer using a technical pen for inked designs. They're easy to use and I feel they give me better control of my linework. I like to apply my patterns for inking with pencil graphite (rub a soft lead pencil on the back of the pattern and then transfer with a stylus) as the ink sometimes balls up on regular transfer paper. Ink the entire outline first, then come back and achieve the detail and dimension with additional inked lines. The closer the lines, the darker the area looks. You can build gradation by using crosshatching in the darkest area. The lines are finer and further apart in the lighter areas. You may also use scattered dots in the light area. Clean the graphite lines off with a small amount of linseed oil or a kneaded eraser after the inking is complete and has had adequate time to dry. Spray with Krylon Matte Finish #1311.

Source
The frame and puffed heart may be ordered from
A Touch of Class by Aileen
11215 Inverness Ct. NE
Albuquerque, NM 87111-7547

Leaf Step by Step

Color Side by Side

1 Apply the dark mixture starting at the base (where the stem comes in) with short, choppy or fuzzy strokes. Pull down the middle of the center vein, tapering out to the tip of the leaf and along the base edge near the stem, forming a T. Pull the dark value to the outside edge of the leaf in at least one area on each side of the leaf (be certain these are not directly opposite each other). The dark area will cover about one-half of the leaf.

2 As you apply the buffing color in one or more areas of the leaf, begin to blend it into the dark area. Generally this is done in one area with only one color. The exception to this is the accent leaf where the buffing color goes all around the dark area to keep it from touching the light area. Sometimes there is more than one buffing color listed on the setup. The additional colors are to be used on the light-, middle- and dark-value leaves. YO is usually used on the light-value leaves, RS on the dark-value leaves. The accent colors like CYD or CRL go on leaves that lead the eye through the design.

3 Block in the remainder of the leaf with the light area mix. Test the color on your painting to be sure you have good contrast and the color is clear and clean. Blend the light area into the buffing and dark areas as you are applying this mixture. Pressure stroke the colors together by pulling straight out from the center vein to the edge of the leaf. Remember, you still want to see your dark values, buffing color and light-area color. Don't overblend.

4 See steps 2–4 of Color on Top of Color for Leaves to create the center vein area, add highlights and refine the leaf.

Color on Top of Color

Color on top of color will speed up the painting time and achieve beautiful results. When using color side by side, the contrast within the leaf is greater.

A ribbon of color is created when brush mixing the colors

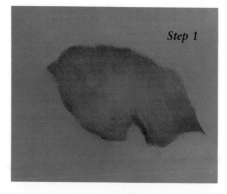

Step 1

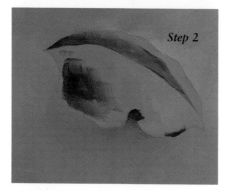

Step 2

Step 3

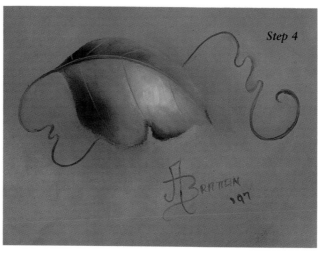

Step 4

used for painting leaves, using color on top of color. Load the brush with PG and pull a large amount of paint to the side or down from the puddle of paint. Load the brush with CL and pull some to one side of the PG puddle. With the brush half on the CL and half on the PG, begin to work the two colors together, making a brighter and lighter green in the center of the ribbon. Continue to work the colors together, making a ribbon of color consisting of at least three values: a dark value on one end, a middle value in the center and a light value on the other end.

1 The entire leaf is blocked in with the proper value (light, medium or dark). Apply the paint with short, choppy strokes. If using more alkyds than oils, use more paint.

2 Change to a size smaller brush, and load the brush with the dark green value plus Blk. Hold the leaf so the small (dark) part is facing you. With pressure on the brush, place the dark triangle of color behind the center vein, pulling to the outside edge. Turn the leaf so the tip is pointed toward you and pull with pressure, forming a slight curve and tapering out to the tip. This dark area creates a resting area for the center vein. The dark always goes behind the curve. The dark area is usually one-third of the leaf and the light area is two-thirds. There are exceptions, but this ratio always produces a beautiful leaf. Place the shading color left in the brush just above the lower back edge on the light side.

The brush may need to be loaded once again with the dark value to have enough paint to shade this area. To obtain a darker shading value for the dark-value leaf, load with the base mixture plus Blk, then PB and then load again with Blk to control the blue. If you see blue when applying the shading, dry wipe the brush and load with YO, which will neutralize the color in the brush. Using very soft, short, choppy strokes, blend these areas.

3 Adding highlights is the next step. They are applied with pressure at the top of the curve of the center vein. With each application, the area becomes smaller and lighter in value. Never start farther than two-thirds of the way up the vein. Always apply the highlights with pressure. Apply the first highlight and then break the bottom edge of the highlight by applying pressure on the bottom edge of the highlight area. The second highlight is applied over the first, breaking the bottom edge of this highlight also. If a third highlight is applied, drop down just a fraction from the center vein area so it is applied in the fullest part of the leaf (where the light is hitting the strongest). Once the highlights are applied, begin the blending process on the back edge of the highlight area by placing the brush half on the highlight and half on the leaf and pulling back toward the base (where the stem comes in) with short, choppy strokes. When this is blended, change the direction of blending by pulling at an angle toward the tip of the leaf. As you blend the lower edge of the highlight, you may need to pull all the way to the edge of the leaf. Whisper the brush over the highlight area very softly. If the highlight needs to be stronger, apply again with a stutter stroke (pressure, lift and pull). This is pulled from the center vein down toward the bottom of the leaf, not the tip. The strongest light shouldn't hit at the center vein but down just a bit. Vary the value of the leaves within the design by not stacking the highlights three times on all leaves.

4 You're now ready to clean up or refine the edges of the leaf. Your leaves will grow a little in this step and you want to be certain all the graphite lines disappear by applying

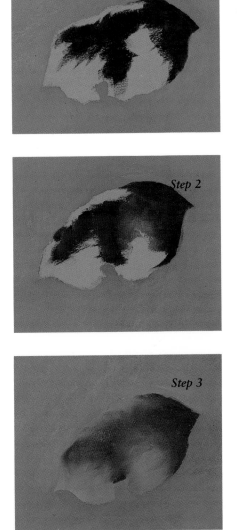

Step 1

Step 2

Step 3

pressure and scrubbing them out. There are many factors to consider in this step: You may add tints (a hint of another color, which helps move the eye through the design area), reinforce lights or darks and deepen or lighten the edges of the leaf according to its position. There are two absolutes you should include on each leaf. One is a dull reflected light (W + Blk) on the dark side of the leaf, at a slight angle from the highlight. This may have to be applied several times, pulling in just a little and then blending between the two colors so you don't lose the dark behind the center vein. The other absolute is a touch of dark under the highlight. Lay a touch of shading color on the surface directly under the highlight area, dry wipe and load your brush with the highlight color, softly pull down and soften into the dark area. Your final blending strokes should be in the direction the secondary veins grow.

Apply the center vein using the chisel edge of a flat brush loaded with a light value. Pull from the base down the dark side of the center vein and then turn and pull the secondary veins from the outside edge in. The other side is pulled from the center vein to the outside. Secondary veins follow the shape of the back edge of the leaf. If veins need to be softened, dry brush over them with a flat brush or mop brush. The vein should appear to go all the way to the edge.

Accent Leaves

Accent leaves are used in the design to add variety, sparkle and to help carry color through the design. The dark area shouldn't be as large as on a green leaf. The buffing color will completely encompass the dark area.

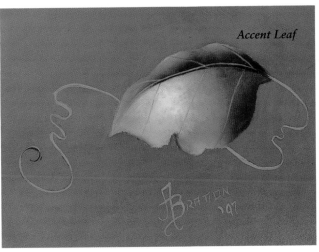

Accent Leaf

Leaf Studies

Leaf Paddle #1

Leaves in the Round

Pattern and instructions on page 45.

Portland Sampler

Pattern and instructions on pages 42-43.

Leaf
Paddle
#2

Leaf
Paddle
#3

See page 44 for instructions for all leaf paddles.

Portland Sampler

Surface Preparation

Sand and seal the sampler board with Designs From the Heart Wood Sealer. Paint the rectangles with Ceramcoat Lichen Grey. Spray lightly with Krylon Matte Finish #1311 and apply pattern. Stain the edges of the board with Winsor & Newton BU and then deepen with BU + Blk. When the painting is finished, very lightly antique the corners of the rectangles and spatter very softly with BU.

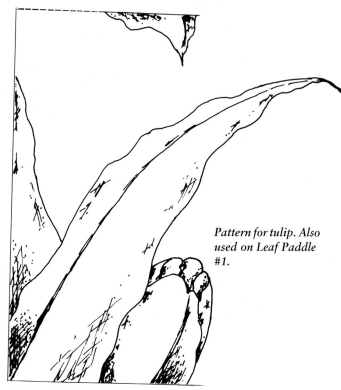

Pattern for tulip. Also used on Leaf Paddle #1.

Pattern for leaves on branch.

Tulip

Light-Value Leaf
Base	Blk + CL + W
Shade	Base mix + Blk
Highlight	W + CL − W
Tint	W + Blk

Dark-Value Leaf
Base	Blk + CL
Shade	Base mix + Blk + (PB)
Highlight	CL + W − W
Tint	W + Blk

Tulip
Dark area	CRL + RS + AC
Buff	CRL + YO
Light area	Dark area mix + NYL + W
Shade	RS + AC + (Blk)
Highlight	NYL + CL + W − W
Tint	W + Blk

Leaves on Branch

Light-Value Leaf
Base	Blk + CL + W
Shade	Base mix + Blk
Highlight	W + (CL) − W
Accent	YO − CRL + RS − AC + RS
Tint	W + Blk

Middle-Value Leaf
Dark area	Blk + CL + (W)
Buff	YO
Light area	Dark area mix + CL + W
Shade	Dark area mix + Blk
Highlight	W + CL − W
Tint	W + Blk

Dark-Value Leaf
Dark area	Blk + CL
Buff	RS
Light area	Dark area mix + CL + W
Shade	Dark area mix + Blk + (PB)
Highlight	W + CL − (YO + W)
Tint	W + Blk

Accent Leaf
Dark area	AC + RS
Buff	CGP + YO
Light area	CGP + W
Shade	Dark area mix + Blk
Highlight	W + CGP − W
Tint	W + Blk

Branch
Dark area	Blk + RS
Light area	CL + W
Shade	Dark area mix + Blk
Highlight	W + CL − W
Tendrils	Shades of green

Apple

Light-Value Leaf

Base	PG + CL + W
Shade	PG + Blk
Highlight	CL + W − W
Accent	CRL + RS − AC + RS − RS
Tint	W + Blk

Dark-Value Leaf

Base	PG + CL + (Blk)
Shade	Base mix + Blk
Highlight	W + CL − W
Accent	RS
Tint	W + Blk

Branch
Same colors as for Leaves on Branch.

Apple

Base	CGP + YO
Shade	PG + RS − (Blk)
Highlight	CGP + W − W
Tint	CYD − W + Blk
Whiskers	RS + Blk − CGP + W

Holly

Light-Value Leaf

Base	PB + CO + YO + CL + W
Shade	Base mix + Blk
Highlight	W + CL − W
Tint	W + Blk

Middle-Value Leaf

Dark area	PB + CO + YO
Buff	RS
Light area	Dark area mix + CL + W
Shade	Dark area mix + Blk
Highlight	W + CL − W
Tint	W + Blk

Dark-Value Leaf

Base	PB + CO
Shade	Base mix + PB + Blk
Highlight	YO + W + (CL)
Tint	W + Blk
Tendrils	Shades of green

Berries

Base	CRL + CO − CRL + AC
Shade	AC + Blk
Highlight	CL + W − W
Tint	W + Blk

Pattern for Apple.

Source

This lovely sampler board may be ordered from
A Touch of Class by Aileen
11215 Inverness Ct. NE
Albuquerque, NM 87111-7547

*Pattern for Holly.
Also used on Leaf
Paddles #1 and #3.*

Leaf Paddles

Surface Preparation

Sand and seal the board with Designs From the Heart Wood Sealer. The top surface is painted with Ceramcoat Ivory. Measure and mark off three squares, allowing 1⅝-inches (4.1cm) between the squares. Apply Scotch Magic transparent tape around the outside of the lines on the top and bottom squares and press the tape down firmly. (Turning one end of each strip of tape under will make it easy to remove.) Leave the middle square on all three paddles Ivory. Paint the top and bottom squares of Paddle #1 with Ceramcoat Lichen Grey. Paint the bottom square on Paddle #2 with Lichen Grey and the top square with Ceramcoat Bonnie Blue plus Ceramcoat Ivory. On Paddle #3, paint the top square with Lichen Grey and the bottom with Blk. You can mix and match any of the patterns from the Portland Sampler on pages 42-43, or the Leaf Study Tray on pages 48-49. After you have finished painting the designs, antique the edges and the heart on the handle with BU. Deepen the antiquing with Blk + BU if needed. Cover the design area and spatter with BU + Blk. The comma stroke/dot border around each square is done with BU + Blk, thinned with a blending medium.

Source

The leaf paddle may be ordered from
A Touch of Class by Aileen
11215 Inverness Ct. NE
Albuquerque, NM 87111-7547

Leaves in the Round

Surface Preparation

Sand and seal the plate with Designs From the Heart Wood Sealer. Paint the center of the plate with Ceramcoat Ivory. Paint the rim of the plate with Ceramcoat Bonnie Blue plus Ivory. Antique and softly spatter the rim with a mixture of PB + Blk + W. If you feel creative, change the color of the rim, then paint the berries to coordinate with the new color scheme.

To paint the light-, middle- and dark-value leaves, as well as the small light leaves, refer to the color setup under Center Leaf Study on page 50.

Accent Leaf

Dark area	DP + RS + Blk
Buff	CGP
Light area	CL + CGP + W
Shade	Dark area mix + Blk
Highlight	CGP + W − W
Tint	W + Blk

Berries

Base	PB + Blk + W
Shade	PB + Blk
Highlight	W
Tint	W + Blk
Whiskers	PB + Blk

 ## Source

This leaf plate can be ordered from
A Touch of Class by Aileen
11215 Inverness Ct. NE
Albuquerque, NM 87111-7547

Leaf Study Tray

Leaf Study Tray

Surface Preparation

Sand and seal the tray with Designs From the Heart Wood Sealer. Paint the entire tray with Ceramcoat Ivory. Mark off each box with graphite and a straightedge. Mask outside the lines around the box you are basecoating with Scotch Magic transparent tape, turning one edge of each strip under for easy removal. With a good brush, apply the following Ceramcoat colors: black acrylic to the lower left and upper right boxes, one part Bonnie Blue plus one part Ivory to the upper left box, one part Seminole Green plus one part Ivory to the lower right box, and Lichen Grey to the center top and center bottom boxes. Leave the center box Ivory. After the basecoat is applied, remove the tape, erase the graphite lines and mist lightly with Krylon Matte finish #1311. When

the painted design is dry, apply BU around the perimeter of the large rectangle and softly blend out with a brush or soft cloth. Antique and very lightly spatter the sides and inner corners of the tray with BU. Create the border around each box with comma strokes and dots, or use a lifeline border as shown in the picture on pages 46-47.

Source

This tray may be ordered from
A Touch of Class by Aileen
11215 Inverness Ct. NE
Albuquerque, NM 87111-7547

Instructions continued on pages 50-51.

Leaf Study Tray

Continued from pages 48-49.

This tray was a delight to design and teach. I believe my students have enjoyed painting this tray as much as anything I have ever taught. I recommend this project for the intermediate student who wants to improve her painting skills. You will be working with color relationships—studying how the different color setups work on different color backgrounds. Notice how the two gray squares appear to be two different colors because of the color of the leaves painted on them— remember, color is relative!

Center Leaf Study

Light-Value Leaf
Dark area	Blk + CL + (W)
Buff	CRL
Light area	Dark area mix + W + (CL)
Shade	Dark area mix + Blk
Highlight	W + (CL) − W
Accent	CRL + RS + (AC)
Tint	W + Blk

Middle-Value Leaf
Dark area	Blk + CL
Buff	YO
Light area	Dark area mix + CL + W
Shade	Dark area mix + Blk
Highlight	W + CL − W
Accent	CRL + RS
Tint	W + Blk

Dark-Value Leaf
Dark area	Blk + CL
Buff	RS
Light area	Dark area mix + CL + W
Shade	Dark area mix + Blk + (PB)
Highlight	W + CL − (YO + W)

Accent Leaf
Dark area	AC + RS + Blk
Buff	CGP
Light area	CGP + W
Shade	Dark area mix + Blk
Highlight	CGP + W + (CL) − W
Tint	W + Blk

Small Light Leaves
Base	Blk + CL + W + (CGP)
Shade	Base mix + Blk
Highlight	W
Tint	W + Blk

Branch
Dark area	Blk + RS
Light area	CL + W
Shade	Dark area mix + Blk
Highlight	CL + W − W

Holly Leaves

Light-Value Leaf
Base	PB + CO + YO + CL + W
Shade	Base mix + Blk
Highlight	CL + W − W
Tint	W + Blk

Middle-Value Leaf
Dark area	PB + CO + YO
Buff	RS
Light area	Dark area mix + CL + W
Shade	Dark area mix + Blk
Highlight	CL + W − W
Tint	W + Blk

Dark-Value Leaf
Base	PB + CO
Shade	Base mix + PB + Blk
Highlight	YO + W + (CL)
Tint	W + Blk

Berries
Base	CRL + CO − CRL + AC
Shade	AC + Blk
Highlight	CL + W − W
Tint	W + Blk

Tulip Leaves

Light-Value Leaf
Base	Blk + CL + W
Shade	Base mix + Blk
Highlight	CL + W − W
Tint	W + Blk

Dark-Value Leaf

Dark area	Blk + CL + (W)
Buff	RS
Light area	Dark area mix + CL + W
Shade	Dark area mix + Blk + (PB)
Highlight	CL + W − W
Tint	W + Blk

Tulip

Dark area	RS + CRL + AC
Buff	CRL + YO
Light area	Dark area mix + NYL + W
Shade	RS + AC + (Blk)
Highlight	NYL + CL − W
Tint	W + Blk

Filler Flowers

Work dark to light: CRL + RS − NYL + CL − W − Touches of Green.

Strawberry Leaves

Light-Value Leaf

Dark area	PB + CO
Buff	CO
Light area	Dark area mix + CL + W
Shade	Dark area mix + Blk
Highlight	CL + W − W
Tint	W + Blk

Middle- and Dark-Value Leaves

Dark area	PB + CO
Buff	YO − RS
Light area	Dark area mix + CL + W − (YO)
Shade	Dark area mix + Blk + PB
Highlight	CL + W + (YO) − W
Accent	CRL + RS − AC + RS
Tint	W + Blk

Strawberries

Base	YO + W + CGP
Shade	CRL + RS + AC
Highlight	CGP + W − CL + W − W
Tint	W + Blk
Seeds	NY + CGP

See Strawberry Step by Step *for instructions for seeds and depressions on page 74.*

Grape Leaves

Leaves

Dark area	YO + Blk
Buff	CL + NYL
Light area	CL + W
Shade	Dark area mix + Blk + PB
Highlight	CL + W − W + (CGP)
Accent	CRL
Tint	W + Blk

Pattern for inked leaves.

Grapes

Dark area	PB + Blk + (AC)
Buff	CRL + AC
Light area	Dark area mix + W
Shade	PB + Blk
Highlight	W + (CL) − W
Tint	W + Blk

Geranium Leaves

Leaves

Dark area	PB + OR
Buff	YO
Light area	Dark area mix + CL + W
Shade	Dark area mix + Blk + (PB)
Highlight	CL + W − W
Tint	W + Blk

Geranium

Base	NYL + CL
Shade	RS + CGP + (Blk)
Highlight	W + CL − W
Accent	CO
Tint	W + Blk
Lines	Blk + RS
Dots	CGP + RS − CL + W

Metallic Gold Leaves

Light-Value Leaves

Dark area	RS
Buff	YO + C
Light area	RG
Shade	BU + Blk
Highlight	G

Middle- and Dark-Value Leaves

Dark area	BU + RS + Blk
Buff	YO + C
Light area	RG
Shade	BU + Blk
Highlight	G

Inked Leaves

Apply the pattern with pencil graphite. Ink the leaves with a technical or crow quill pen. When the ink has dried completely, erase the graphite lines with a kneaded eraser. Spray with Krylon Matte Finish #1311. Tint with BU thinned with a glazing medium and softly pull the paint out.

Flips, Ruffles, Pleats and Folds

Most floral, fruit and leaf designs will have some flips, ruffles, pleats and folds for you to paint. Fabrics and ribbons also have flips, ruffles, pleats and folds. When properly executed, these elements create the illusion of depth and dimension in the painting. Refer to the following step-by-step instructions anytime you need help painting these elements.

Creating Flips With Color on Top of Color

1 Lightly basecoat the main area of the object and the flip. You may wish to leave a small line visible between the flip and body so the pattern lines aren't lost.

2 Pick up the shading color on a small flat brush, apply with pressure at both ends of the flip, and in the areas where there are indentations in the flip. When applying this shading, the chisel edge of the brush should stay against the edge of the flip. Don't outline the flip with the shading color because this makes the shadow area all the same value. Dry wipe your brush, place it half on the edge of the shading under the flip and half on the main body and soften the shading color under the flip into the base color of the petal to create several values. If your instructions have a shading color plus another color in parentheses, now is the time to pick up the optional darker color in parentheses. Place this second-value dark at both ends of the flip and in several of the indented areas under the flip.

3 Place a touch of dark in the center of the back, outside edge of the flip. If this flip has another element under it, place the shading color just inside the edge so that a touch of light is still on the outside edge. This touch of dark shading is necessary to make the flip roll. Blend as instructed in the above step.

4 Pick up the highlight colors and apply with pressure on the most prominent areas closest to the light source. Apply the highlight across the indented area. This will create more dimension. If you don't have several value changes on your flip, go one step lighter by applying a lighter value on the larger indented areas. Edge-blend the outside edge of the highlight using a small flat brush. Begin blending by placing the brush half on the edge of the highlight and half on the flip. Dry wipe often, then lightly soften over the entire flip area. The final step is to take the chisel edge of your brush loaded with highlight color and pull this light color so it connects to the body of the petal.

Creating Flips With Color Side by Side

1 Place the dark-area color under the flip at both ends, in the indentations and a small amount in the middle of the outside edge of the flip. As you block in these areas, concentrate on applying the color more heavily at the ends of the flip and in the more prominent indented areas.

2 Block in the remainder of the flip and petal with the light-area mix. Use pressure to blend the colors together. When the hard, definite line is broken, whisper the brush lightly over the top to soften.

3 Load the brush with the shading color and apply, with pressure, at both ends of the flip, in the darker indented areas and on the middle of the back edge of the flip. Blend these areas into the body, leaving them where they were placed. If several values are not present within your dark area, add a second-value dark at this time.

4 Refer to step 4 on Creating Flips With Color on Top of Color for application of highlights.

Creating Ruffles Using Color on Top of Color

1 Block in the entire area with your base mixture. Load your brush with the shading color. Turn your work so the chisel edge of the brush may be placed on the furthest outside edge of the petal. Pressure the color into the petal. If needed, apply a second-value dark on some of these edges. Some of the darks should be pulled farther into the petals than others. When blending these dark areas, don't create hard, definite lines that produce a funnel or tornado effect. The darks are blended in all directions.

2 Apply the first highlight color with pressure across the top of the raised area by placing the side of the brush on the edge and pulling across the petal. The first highlight may cover most of the area. Apply the second highlight, which is lighter and smaller, on top of the first highlight. You may not wish to stack each highlight equally, so that a value change is created. On some ruffles, stack the highlight a third time with pure white color. Blend these highlights into the petal by placing your brush half on the highlight and half on the base color and blending with short, choppy strokes. The strongest light should not always be on the edge of the ruffle; on some ruffles, let the strongest light fall inside the petal. If the light is on the outside edge, it relates a sharp, crisp feeling. When it's on the inside, it portrays a soft, full, rounded look. Variation is the spice of beautiful painting.

Creating Ruffles Using Color Side by Side

1 Apply the dark-area color in the areas protuding the farthest, using the chisel edge of the brush on the outside edge of the petal. As you pull into the petal, make your strokes rough and hacky. Apply the light area mix over the remainder of the petal, blending it with the dark area mix as you do so. Dry wipe and blend the two colors together, leaving the stronger color on the edge. Load your brush with the shading color and turn your work so you can comfortably place the chisel edge of the brush on the outside edge of the petal. Pressure the shading color into the petal. Dry wipe and apply the second-value dark on some of the deepened areas. Dry wipe and blend by placing the brush half on the dark area and half on the base of the petal.

2 For highlights refer to the instructions for applying highlights on the ruffles using color on top of color.

Continued on page 54.

Color on Top of Color

Flips
1
2
3

Pleats
1
2
3

4

3

Folds
2
1

Ruffles
2
1

Color Side by Side

Flips
1
2
3

4

3

Folds
2
1

Pleats
1
2
3

Ruffles
2
1

Flips, Ruffles, Pleats and Folds

Continued from page 52.

Creating Pleats Using Color on Top of Color

1 Apply the base mixture using very little paint. Leave it rough and hacky. You may wish to leave a visible line so you'll know where to place the darks.

2 Load the brush with the shading color. Turn your work so the chisel edge of the brush is on the outside edge of the petal. Apply the shading color by pulling color with pressure down one side of the pleat line. Go back and make this dark area larger in one small area. Dry wipe and place your brush half on the dark and half on the base mixture and softly blend the shading color into the base color. Apply second-value darks (deeper color) on top of the original shading in a smaller area, usually on the outside edge. Dry wipe and blend.

3 Apply the first highlight by placing the brush on the outside edge and pulling down the side of the dark area. Pressure some of the highlight out into the petal so the highlight area becomes wider at the fullest point and you haven't created a line against a line. Stack this highlight at least one more time with a lighter value. Apply this highlight with pressure in the area where the strongest light is hitting. Blend the outside edge of the highlight, dry wipe and lightly soften over the area.

Creating Pleats Using Color Side by Side

1 Apply the dark-area mix to the outside edge of the petal, starting where the petal extends farthest, then pull down the underneath side of the hard, definite line or pleat. This area should be larger at one point so you don't create a line against a line. The outside edge of the dark should be applied with short, choppy strokes so that when you apply the light area mix, the blending process begins by pulling the light into the dark.

2 Please refer to the directions for pleats using color on top of color for the shading and highlights.

Creating Folds Using Color on Top of Color

Folds are different than ruffles, pleats and flips, so before you begin to paint one, you should practice drawing the shape of a fold. Refer to the pattern lines shown in step 1 of Folds Using Color on Top of Color on page 53. Once you can successfully draw these lines, you will be able to paint a realistic fold. If in the painting process you lose the fold, take your stylus and draw it back in over the wet paint.

1 With pressure, block in the area with the base mixture, applying very little paint. Leave the graphite lines showing faintly so you can see where to place the darks and lights.

2 With pressure, load a small flat brush with the shading mixture. Apply the shading mixture in the areas as illustrated on page 52. Soften the outside edges of these areas into the base of the petal. One edge remains definite and the other edge should be blended into the base of the petal. Apply second-value darks in some areas as shown. Very softly blend the outer edges of the dark areas, being careful not to lose them or to destroy the shape.

3 Load your small brush with the first highlight color and apply with pressure in the areas receiving the strongest light and needing to be lifted. The main, top highlight should be applied by placing the chisel edge of the brush on the hard, definite line and pulling across the top of the fold. Pressure stroke this color out onto the petal. Apply a highlight one value lighter in a smaller area on top of the previous one. It may be necessary to build this highlight even one step lighter. When applying the highlight on the inside part, take the chisel edge of your brush and connect the light edge (very thin) to the dark area, just as you connected the top of the flip to the body of the petal. Very lightly blend these highlights out.

Creating Folds Using Color Side by Side

1 Place the dark area mix in the areas as illustrated, or in the same areas that shading was applied in the step for Creating Folds Using Color on Top of Color.

2 Place the light area mix in the remaining areas and blend between the colors, being careful not to lose the shape.

3 Place the shading and highlight colors on the fold as illustrated and described in the steps for Creating a Fold Using Color on Top of Color.

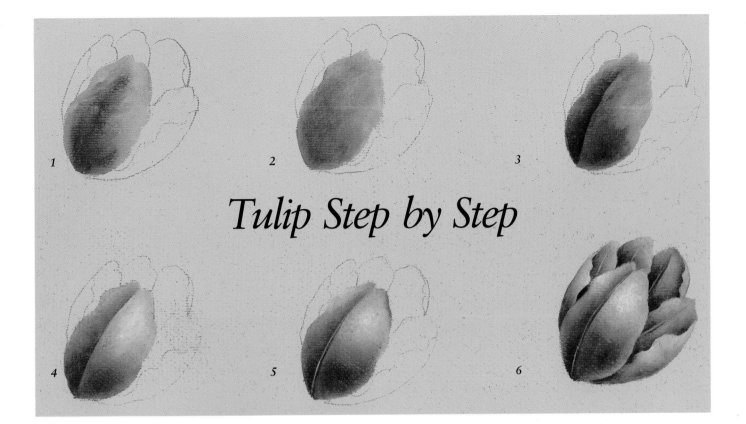

Tulip Step by Step

The same method for painting leaves is used for painting the tulip because it has a cervix or center vein area in each petal. This area should be developed on the center petal of the tulip more strongly than the other petals.

1 Load a flat brush with the dark mixture and apply at the base. With pressure, pull the paint down the middle of the center vein area. This will form a T area on the petal. Use very little paint and leave the edges of the area rough and hacky. Dry wipe the brush and pick up the buffing color. As you are applying the buffing color with pressure, pull into the dark area and start the blending process. The buffing color is applied all around the dark-area mix. Dry wipe and load the brush with the light-area color and block in the remainder of the petal, working into the buffing color. It's important that as you go from one color mix to the next, some of the first color is still in the brush.

2 Pressure-stroke the colors together by placing the brush at the center vein and pulling straight out to the edge of the petal. Don't overblend. You should still see all three mixtures. Remove any hard, definite lines.

3 Load a smaller brush with the shading mixture. Turn your work, place the dark triangle of color behind the center vein, then turn the petal with the tip pointed toward you and pull with pressure, forming a slight curve and tapering out toward the tip. Place the shading color left in the brush on the other lower edge of the light side. Using very soft, short, choppy strokes, blend these areas.

4 The strongest light will hit where the petal appears to be the fullest. The highlights will be stacked: With each application, the area becomes smaller and the color lighter in value. Begin the first application about one-half to two-thirds of the way down the vein. As the first highlight is applied, pres-

sure it out into the petal to develop a fuller feeling. Stack the highlight as many times as necessary for the desired effect. Dry wipe and begin the blending process by placing the brush half on the highlight and half on the tulip and pulling back toward the base with short, choppy strokes. Dry wipe your brush and change the angle so you're pulling toward the tip of the tulip. You may need to pull all the way to the outside edge of the tulip. Dry wipe and softly whisper the brush over the remainder of the highlight. If it needs to be stronger, apply again with a stutter stroke (pressure, lift and pull). The strongest light should not be at the center vein, but out away from it.

5 Use primarily light values to clean up the edges. Develop a reflected light on the dark side at an angle to or opposite the highlight. This may need to be applied several times to develop a rounded, full feeling on that side. Your final blending—which refines the tulip—is in the growth direction. Apply the center vein using the chisel edge of a flat brush loaded with a light to middle value. Pull from the base down the dark side of the center vein. Some tulips have a darker accent color at the tip. Place the lightest value first with this being the largest area. Apply a deeper dark on top. Blend the outside edge of the first dark by placing your brush half on the tulip and half on the dark. When this is blended, dry wipe and soften over the top of the other dark.

6 The remainder of the tulip petals are developed by placing the dark-area color in the shadow areas and down the middle of the center vein area. The buffing color is pulled into this color and the remainder of the petal is blocked in with the light area. Pressure-stroke the colors together. Shade and develop the center vein area if the petal has one. Apply highlights, stacking them as required. They will probably not need to be as strong as they are on the top petal of the top tulip.

A Tulip for You

Surface Preparation

Rub the wooden surface of the mirror with Titanium White alkyd or oil. If this seems dry, pick up a touch of Winsor & Newton Blending and Glazing Medium to make it move more easily. When this is dry, spray lightly with Krylon Matte #1311 before applying the pattern. If you are painting this design on a different surface, sand, seal and apply a wash or opaque basecoat of Ceramcoat Ivory or Ceramcoat Medium Flesh for the background.

Tulip

Dark area	AC + CRL + RS
Buff	CYD + YO
Light area	Mix + NYL
Shade	Mix + (Blk)
Highlight	NYL + W − W

Leaves

Base	Blk + CL + W
Shade	Base mix +
	Blk + (PB)
Highlight	CL + W − W
Accent	RS + (CRLT) − YO

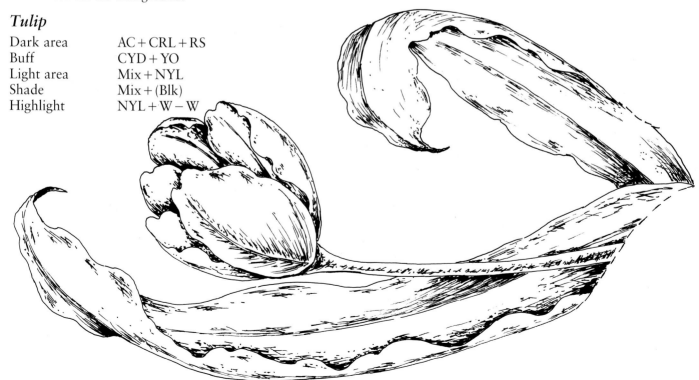

Tulips for a Victorian Fire Screen

Surface Preparation

Glue chip glass requires no preparation. If the surface is too slick, spray it with Krylon Matte Finish #1311. Tape a line drawing of the pattern to a piece of cardboard and secure the glass over the pattern. Sand and seal the wood with Designs From the Heart Wood Sealer and then basecoat it with Ceramcoat Village Green. Spray lightly with Krylon Matte Finish #1311 before applying the pattern to the wooden base. Silver leaf the rim of the base and spindles over Red Iron Oxide acrylic. Antique with BU. More explicit instructions for silver and gold leaf may be found on page 8.

White Tulips

Dark area	OC + PG + RS
Light area	NYL + W
Shade	Dark area mix + Blk
Highlight	CL + W − W
Tint	RS − CYD

Yellow Tulips

Dark area	YO + CYD
Light area	CL + NYL
Shade	CYD − CRL + RS + (Blk + OC)
Tint	W + Blk

Leaves

Base	PG + CL + W + (Blk) + (OC)
Shade	Base mix + Blk + (PB)
Highlight	W + CL − W
Tint	W + Blk

Scrolls

Paint with green mixtures from leaves, then highlight with W + CL. Tint tips with CYD.

Lilacs

Thin the paint with a medium such as Winsor & Newton Blending and Glazing Medium and use a small, round brush, working dark to light: OC + Blk − RS − CYD − NYL − W.

Pattern for base.

Tulips for a Victorian Fire Screen

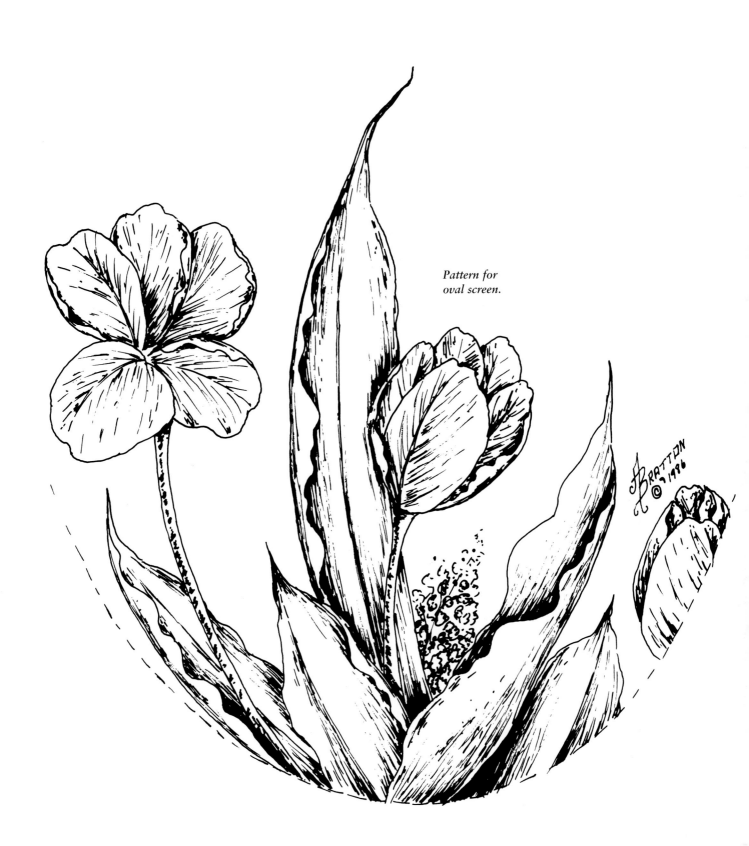

Pattern for
oval screen.

Plum Beautiful &
A Swan's Delight

Pattern and instructions for Plum Beautiful *on pages 62-63,* A Swan's Delight *on pages 64-65.*

Plum Step by Step

The basic shape of the plum is a sphere, but there is also a plunge line or crevice that must be dealt with. There are several ways to treat this area. Plums can be developed using color side by side or color on top of color. Plums have a frosted look created by leaving the paint blotchy and rough. This is much easier to create by glazing on the stronger darks, highlights and dull reflected light. This plum was developed with an upper right light source.

1 With pressure, apply the dark-area mix in the crescent area and next to the plunge line, using very short, choppy strokes. The dark area or crescent must go one-half to two-thirds of the way around the plum. The crescent will turn at the top and follow the plunge line about half to two-thirds of the way down, and taper out. This dark does not touch the plunge line, it is placed just below it. The lower part of the crescent may touch the outside edge of the plum in the original block-in, or it can be placed just inside the outside edge. The dark area will block in half of the plum since it's such a dark pigment color.

2 The plunge line can also be created by placing the dark on the outside edge of the small side of the plum. The dark or crescent on the front side will touch the front edge of the plunge line.

3 Dry wipe your brush, load with the buffing color or colors, and place it next to the dark area (pull one into the other) in several areas where you would like a sparkle of color. If the buffing color completely surrounds the dark area in this plum it can create too much color.

4 Dry wipe, but while still carrying some of the dark area color, load your brush with NYL + W and block in the remainder of the plum. Pressure-stroke between the colors, leaving the colors in the areas where they were placed. Work only between the colors. The frosted look is achieved by leaving the paint rough and hacky.

5 At this stage the plum could be left to dry. The darks and highlights can be glazed on when dry, or can be applied wet on wet. Strengthen the dark area on the crescent with the shading color in the lower portion of the crescent, at the upper portion where it turns and a portion of the dark area behind the plunge line. Place these on with pressure and just barely edge-blend. If the plunge line was created by placing light on the small side of the plunge, the dark area on the outside edge should be deepened in one area to create a value change.

6 Load the brush with the first highlight and place these on with pressure. Place these highlights in the fattest, fullest area where the light is strongest, as well as on the top side of the plunge line. If the light area is behind the plunge, place a highlight in one small area. Dry wipe and strengthen the areas with the strongest light. This could be repeated two more times if the plum is in an area that requires a very strong light. Dry wipe your brush and place the brush half on the base and half on the highlight and, with pressure, pull one into the other. When this is blended, dry wipe and soften over the top of the highlight. The dull reflected light is then applied with a mixture of W + Blk. These are placed on the outside edge, pulling into the fruit farther in one area so as not to create a line or halo around an edge. If the plum is resting on a surface, the reflected light will not hit in the area where it is resting. The tint, if needed, can be added at this time. If the buffing color has remained strong, you may wish to omit this step. If needed, load a brush and softly blot before applying in a middle-value area. Soften over the top of this blending in every direction.

Light-Value Blossom

Base	BC + NYH + NYL
Shade	BC + DP + (Blk)
Highlight	NYR + NYL + W − W
Accent	BC

Middle-Value Blossom

Dark area	BC + DP + Blk
Buff	Dark area mix + NYH
Light area	NYR + NYL + W
Shade	Dark area mix + Blk
Highlight	NYR + NYL + W − W
Accent	BC + AC

Dark-Value Blossom

Base	BC + DP + Blk
Shade	Base mix + Blk
Highlight	NYH + NYR − NYL

Blossom Center

Base	YO + NY
Shade	BC + DP + Blk
Highlight	W + CL − W
Dark lines	BC + DP + Blk
Splotches	BC + DP + Blk
	Dark area mix +
	NYH + NYR

Plum Beautiful

Surface Preparation

Spray the wooden surface of the tray lightly with Krylon Matte #1311 and apply the pattern lightly. The same effect could be achieved on another surface by applying a wash of Ceramcoat Ivory or staining the surface with W + NYL. When the painting is dry, spray lightly with Krylon Matte #1311. Mix Winsor & Newton Blending and Glazing Medium with a mixture of W + Blk + BC and apply in the deeper triangle areas around the design. Work this into the background. If this rouging of the background is done several times, it gives more depth to the background.

Light-Value Plum

Dark area	DP + PB + BC + Blk
Buff	AC + CRL
Light area	Dark area mix + NYL + W
Shade	Dark area mix + Blk
Highlight	NYL + W − W
Tint	W + Blk − BC + AC

Middle-Value Plum

Dark area	DP + PB + BC + Blk
Light area	Dark area mix + NYL + W
Shade	Dark area mix + Blk
Highlight	NYL + W − W
Tint	W + Blk − BC + AC

Dark-Value Plum

Base	PB + Blk + W
Shade	Base mix + Blk
Highlight	NYL + W
Tint	W + Blk − DP + BC

Light-Value Leaves

Base	CL + Blk + W
Shade	Base mix + Blk
Highlight	W + CL − W
Tint	YO − W + Blk

Middle-Value Leaves

Base	CL + Blk + W
Shade	Base mix + Blk + (PB)
Highlight	W + CL − W
Tint	RS − W + Blk

Dark-Value Leaves

Base	Blk + CL + (W)
Shade	Base mix + PB
Highlight	YO + W + (CL)
Tint	W + Blk

Branch

Dark area	Blk + RS
Light area	Dark area mix + CL + W
Shade	Dark area mix + Blk
Highlight	W + CL − W

A Swan's Delight

Surface Preparation

If you plan to put grosgrain ribbon around the base of the swan as shown on page 60, gently pull the canvas band off. Lightly sand the head and body with #400 or #600 sandpaper. Basecoat the canvas body and head with Ceramcoat Ivory. If the beak needs to be reshaped, do so with black acrylic. Spray lightly with Krylon Matte #1311 before applying the pattern. Rouge touches of black and white around the design after it's painted, then work touches of YO and the mixture of AC + DP + NY + Blk into the edges of the W + Blk. Add Winsor & Newton Blending and Glazing Medium to the paint so it's easier to move. Rubbing in a circular motion using a soft rag will help to remove hard, definite lines. The rouge is applied several times to give additional depth. Use Damar Varnish on the canvas areas to keep the paint from cracking and pulling off. The head of the swan may be finished with a water-base varnish such as Right Step.

Mauve Plum and Tulip

Dark area	AC + DP + Blk
Buff	CRL + NY
Light area	Dark area mix + NYR + NYL
Shade	Dark area mix + Blk + (OC)
Highlight	NYL + W – W
Tint	W + Blk

Green Gage Plum

Dark area	OC + Blk
Buff	Dark area mix + NYR
Light area	Buff mix + NYL
Shade	Dark area mix + AC + DP + Blk
Highlight	NYL + W – W
Tint	W + Blk

White Tulips

Dark area	PG + RS + CGP + (Blk)
Light area	NYL + W
Shade	Dark area mix + Blk
Highlight	NYL + W – W
Tint	CRL + NYR + NY – DP + AC + NYH + (B

Color on the petal tips is added after the tulip is dry. The light color is applied first and the darker color is added on top.

Leaves

Base	PG + CL + W + (Blk)
Shade	Base mix + Blk + (PB)
Highlight	CL + W – W
Tint	W + Blk – OC + W – AC + DP + NY + Blk

Bronze Fruit

Pattern and instructions on pages 68-69.

Bronze Fruit Step by Step

This blending technique will require both pressure and a very soft touch. It is also a lesson in values and how they build shape and give dimension.

1 In painting the Bronze Fruit, the side-by-side color technique is used on all the objects. Place the dark value on all the objects. Block them in with rough, choppy strokes.

2 Block in the remainder of each object with the light value and blend. Place the brush, with pressure, half on the dark and half on the light area and blend with short, choppy strokes. Remove the hard, definite lines and begin to build a middle value. Remember to blend the lower part of the crescent across the width of the element.

3 Place the shading color on each object and lightly blend until the dark areas are softened. There should be a dark value within the dark areas as well as a middle- and light-value area.

4 Place the highlights on each object. Apply them with pressure, stacking several on top of each other. The highlight on the apple will be the strongest. Blend around the outside edge of the highlights and then softly over the top to soften them. The leaves are painted with the color setups for the apple, pear and grapes, just using the steps for the regular leaves.

Bronze Fruit

Pattern for side of tin.

Surface Preparation

To prepare the tin, refer to the instructions for preparing tin on page 8. Spray the tin with Krylon Antique White Interior/Exterior Enamel. The scrollwork is done with BU. When dry, antique and splatter outside the scrollwork with BU.

Sand and seal the wooden surface with Designs From the Heart Wood Sealer. Paint the inside surface of the board with Ceramcoat Flesh Tan. Stain all the other edges with BU. Deepen the edges with BU + Blk. Spatter with BU + Blk, keeping the spatters out of the main design area.

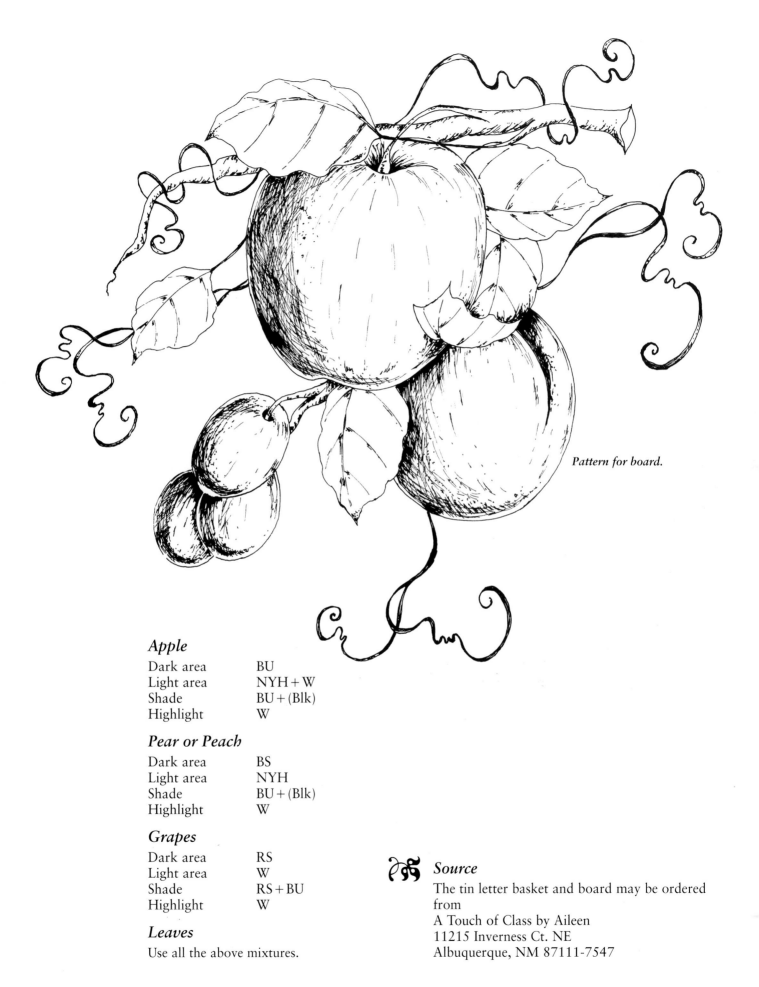

Pattern for board.

Apple

Dark area	BU
Light area	NYH + W
Shade	BU + (Blk)
Highlight	W

Pear or Peach

Dark area	BS
Light area	NYH
Shade	BU + (Blk)
Highlight	W

Grapes

Dark area	RS
Light area	W
Shade	RS + BU
Highlight	W

Leaves

Use all the above mixtures.

Source

The tin letter basket and board may be ordered from
A Touch of Class by Aileen
11215 Inverness Ct. NE
Albuquerque, NM 87111-7547

Potpourri Pansies

Pattern and instructions on pages 72-73.

Pansy Step by Step

The first step to painting a pansy is to understand the anatomy of the flower. The pansy consists of five petals. The front petal is the largest. It contains dark lines, a face and a throat. These are the last details added to the flower. The two middle petals are between the front petal and the back two petals. These petals generally have dark lines on them, but sometimes they don't. The dark-line area can be large or quite small, heart-shaped or rounded.

The yellow face is easier to apply after the dark-line area is dry, but if you do it wet-on-wet, the effect will be nicer because it's difficult to cover the dry, dark lines with a light yellow mixture. If you do work wet-on-wet, remember to load the brush with the face mixture and dry wipe the brush each time you pull down into the dark before reloading with the light yellow. The throat is a fine, thin line of Cadmium Red Light that lies at the top of the face. Apply it with a liner brush loaded with Cadmium Red Light plus a medium such as Winsor & Newton's paint thinner for alkyds or Blending and Glazing Medium for oils.

The back petals seldom have dark lines, but occasionally you'll find dark lines on some of them. Remember there are exceptions to all of these statements in nature.

Pansies come in just about any color combination you can imagine, so don't be afraid to create the pansy of your imagination. A pansy has a velvety feel, and this is created by leaving the paint rough and hacky.

1 This pansy was painted using color on top of color, but color side by side could have been used to create stronger contrasts in the pansy. Block in the front and middle petals with a mixture of NYL + NYH + CRL. Apply this mixture with pressure to the petals using a scant amount of paint if using oils, and a heavier covering if using alkyds. You may wish to leave a thin line unpainted between the petals and flips. Don't place this base mix in the dark-line areas but be certain a narrow line of this base mixture is pulled around the dark-line area to the throat area on each side.

2 Load a small, flat brush with a mixture of IR + BC and apply with pressure in the ruffle areas and the pleat. Refer to the step-by-step instructions for ruffles and pleats on pages 52-54 for more detailed instructions. Dry wipe your brush and place half on the inside edge of the dark and half on the base mix and pull, with pressure, one into the other until the hard, definite line is bro-

ken. Let up on the pressure and soften over the area. Don't overblend. When placing the shading on the middle petals behind the front petal, make it heavier in places and lighter in others. Blend this as previously instructed. Look at the shading areas. If you don't see at least two dark values in the shadow areas, deepen some of them again with IR + BC + BU and blend.

3 Apply the first highlight with pressure using NYL + W. On some of the highlight areas apply a stronger highlight with pure white. Each time a highlight is applied it is smaller in area and lighter in value. Blend the outside edge of the highlight first, then dry wipe and soften back over the area very lightly. If you have lost your middle value or you wish the pink tones to be more prevalent, apply a small amount of CRL in the middle value areas and blend softly. Remember, just a little goes a long way!

4 Block in the back petals with the base mixture of AC + BC + IR, leaving the pattern line unpainted between the middle petals and the folds. These colors can be difficult to work with as they are transparent and they slip and slide. You

Continued on page 72.

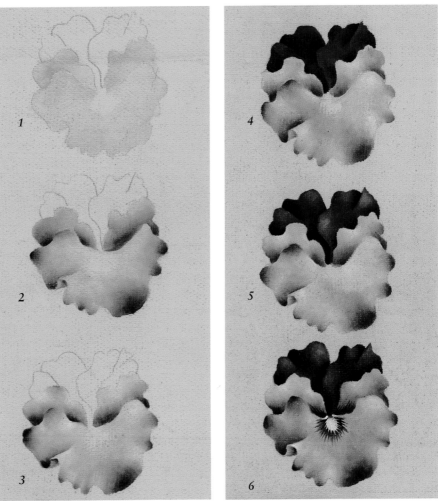

Pansy Step by Step

Continued from page 71.

can adjust your mixture by adding more IR or letting it sit a few minutes before applying the shading colors.

You can also block them in and glaze in the shading and highlight colors. Apply the shading colors of AC + BC + IR + BU to the dark areas. Blend and reevaluate. If the dark areas need to be darker, pick up a tad more BU and deepen some of the areas.

5 Apply the first highlight of CRL + NYH to the light areas. Place a lighter highlight of the above mix + NYL on top of the first highlight on some of the others. Blend these out. Refer to the step-by-step instructions for folds on page 54 if you need more help in developing the folds on these back petals.

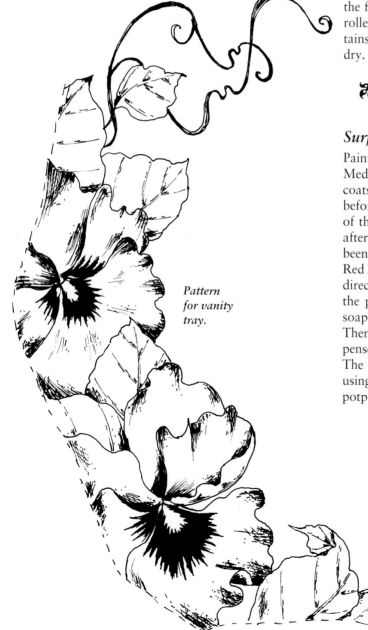

Pattern for vanity tray.

6 With a small flat brush, apply BC + AC + IR + BU in the dark line areas, avoiding the face area. You may use the chisel edge of a small flat brush or you may be able to work better with a liner. If using a liner, use a touch of a medium such as Winsor & Newton's paint thinner for alkyds or Blending and Glazing Medium for oils. Pull this dark color out into the petal so that, as it leaves the dark area, it forms a triangle area and comes to a fine point. These lines must flow with the direction of the petal. The yellow face is done the same way; just be certain to dry wipe and load the brush with the yellow mixture before pulling the lines out. Apply the throat with a liner brush using CRL at the top of the yellow line area. The final step is to add two white comma strokes that lie half on the front petal and half on the middle petals. These create a rolled area that holds all the petals together. If the pansy contains dark color in this area, apply them after the painting is dry.

Surface Preparation

Paint the lid with a mixture of Ceramcoat Fleshtone and Medium Flesh. Apply several coats, wet sanding between coats as necessary. Spray lightly with Krylon Matte #1311 before applying the pattern. Gold leaf the edges and the back of the lid. This may be done before painting the design or after the design is dry and several coats of matte spray have been applied to the painted design. Apply the gold leaf over Red Iron Oxide and very lightly antique with BU. For explicit directions on applying gold leaf, refer to page 8. To prepare the porcelain vanity tray and lotion dispenser, wash with soap and water and mist lightly with Krylon Matte #1311. Then apply the pattern lightly and begin to paint. The dispenser and the edge of the vanity tray are also gold leafed. The pansies on the vanity tray and dispenser were painted using the same color setups as were used on the pansy on the potpourri holder, but with varied placement of colors.

Potpourri Pansies

Front and Middle Petals

Base	NYL + NYH + CRL
Shade	IR + BC + (BU)
Highlight	NYL + W − W
Accent	CRL
Dark lines	BC + AC + IR + (BU)
Face	CL + NYH + W
Throat	CRL
Rolled area	W

Back Petals

Base	AC + BC + IR
Shade	Base mix + BU
Highlight	CRL + NYH − NYL

Leaves

Base	CL + Blk + (W)
Shade	Base mix + Blk + (PB)
Highlight	CL + W − W
Tint	RS − BC + IR

Pattern for potpourri holder.

From this basic leaf color setup, you can paint all the leaves in the design. Mix three values—a light value, middle value and a dark value. When mixing the dark values, you might wish to omit the white. To shade the dark-value leaves, use PB with the mix plus Blk. When applying the first highlight on the light-value leaf, omit the CL and start with a dirty brush + W if the base color is a clear, clean green. If the green is not clear, add a touch of CL. For further information, refer to the leaf step by step on pages 38-39.

Pattern for lotion dispenser.

Strawberry Step by Step

1

2

3

4

Everyone loves strawberries, and I've provided projects for every skill level: The strawberry pattern for the jelly jar lid on page 78 is an excellent pattern for beginners. The pattern for the cream pitcher is a good project for intermediate painters. The puzzle shown on page 40 should challenge everyone because of the black background. Most strawberries—except for the very light, new berries—are developed using color side by side. When developing the strawberry, you are developing a modified spherical or round shape with an upper right light source.

1 With pressure, load your brush with a mixture of CRM + AC + RS. Place this color in the shadow areas. Apply the first buffing color of CRL + YO around the shadow area and blend. Apply the second buffing color of CYD + NY around the first. Pull the two colors together with short, choppy strokes. Block in the remainder of the strawberry with the dirty brush (leaving a little of the paint from the previous step in the brush) plus NYL.

2 Blend between the colors, exerting pressure to remove the hard, definite lines. To blend the lower portion of the crescent, blend across the width of the berry. Load your brush with the shading color and apply in the darkest shadow areas. Place your brush half on the shadow and half on the base and blend these colors with short, choppy strokes.

3 Stack the highlight in the upper right quadrant, first with W + CL and then with a lighter value. Blend around the edges of the highlight and then touch lightly all over. Place a dull, reflected light of W + Blk on the left outside edge and softly blend in.

4 Use a round brush loaded with Winsor & Newton's Blending and Glazing Medium and the appropriate color for applying the seeds and depressions they lie in. There are two methods you can use for placing the seeds on the strawberry. One is to make the depression with a darker value than the area on which it will be placed, using NYH + CGP to place a seed in each depression. The seeds and depressions should follow the contour of the strawberry. Don't place too many on the berry. The second method is to apply the seeds and then to make the depression by placing a deeper color around the seed with a liner brush. After the seeds are applied, the texture is added with W, starting in the highlight area and working around the seeds, leaving only pressure marks in the medium- and dark-value areas.

Bract

1 Block in the entire bract with a middle-value green (Blk + CL + W). As you start to develop the bract, remember it is one piece at the stem and then develops into leaflike tips. Create a deep, dark cavity from which the stem will emerge. Highlight in front of this with W + CL.

2 Place highlights on the outside edge of each leaf tip with W + CL. Stack W highlights on top of the more prominent tips.

3 Pull the stem down into the dark cavity. Study the illustration and place several highlights on the stem.

 Source

The pitcher may be ordered from
A Touch of Class by Aileen
11215 Inverness Ct. NE
Albuquerque, NM 87111-7547

Strawberries and Cream

Strawberries

Dark area	AC + RS + CRM
Buff	YO + CRM
Light area	Dark area mix + NYL
Shade	Dark area mix + (Blk)
Highlight	NYL + W − W
Tint	W + Blk

Small Berry

Base	NYL
Tint	CGP + (PG)
Shade	AC + RS + CRM
Highlight	W

See **Strawberry Step by Step** *for instructions for seeds and depressions on page 74.*

Blossom

Dark area	CGP + PG + (RS)
Light area	NYL + W
Shade	Dark area mix + PG
Highlight	W + CL − W
Tint	RS

Leaves

Dark area	PG + CL + W
Buff	YO − RS
Light area	Dark area mix + CL + W
Shade	Dark area mix + Blk
Highlight	W + CL − W
Tint	W + Blk − AC + RS + CRM

Surface Preparation

Porcelain is a lovely surface to paint on. Lightly mist the porcelain with Krylon Matte #1311 before lightly applying the pattern. Gold leaf the edges following the instructions on page 8. Paint the border with a light green mixture of Blk + CL + W, adding touches of red to the ends of the scrolls. When the scrollwork is dry, place a light green mix thinned with Winsor & Newton Blending and Glazing Medium next to the scrollwork and move out onto the surface with a brush. Using a soft cloth, rub the edge of this light green mixture in a circular motion until it's blended into the background of the porcelain. Spatter the antiqued area with this same light green mixture.

Pattern and instructions for single strawberry on page 78.

Pattern for top of puzzle.

Light- to Middle-Value Strawberries

Dark area	AC + CRM + RS
Buff	Dark area mix + CYD + (YO)
Light area	Buff mix + CL + NYL
Shade	AC + Blk
Highlight	NYL + CL − W
Tint	CGP − W + Blk

Medium- to Dark-Value Strawberries

Dark area	AC + RS + DP
Buff	AC + YO + CRM
Light area	Buff mix + CO + NYL
Shade	AC + Blk + DP
Highlight	NYL + CL − W + CL
Tint	W + Blk − CGP

Unripened Berries

Base	NYL + CGP + (Blk)
Shade	CO − AC + CRM − CGP + Blk
Highlight	W

> *See* **Strawberry Step by Step** *for instructions for seeds and depressions on page 74.*

Light-Value Leaves

Dark area	PB + CO + YO
Buff	CYD
Light area	Dark area mix + CL + W
Shade	Dark area mix + Blk
Highlight	CL + W − W
Tint	W + Blk

Middle and Dark Leaves

Dark area	PB + CO
Buff	YO + RS
Light area	Dark area mix + CL + W − (YO)
Shade	Dark area mix + Blk + PB
Highlight	W + CL + (YO) − (W)
Accent	CRM + RS − AC + RS
Tint	W + Blk

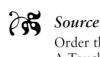 ## Source

Order this puzzle from
A Touch of Class by Aileen
11215 Inverness Ct. NE
Albuquerque, NM 87111-7547

Surface Preparation

Sand and seal the surface with Designs From the Heart Wood Sealer. Stain the outside of the strawberry puzzle with BU. Deepen the bottom edge with BU + Blk. Lightly spatter with BU + Blk. Paint the inside and the puzzle pieces with Ceramcoat Black acrylic.

Pattern for bottom of puzzle.

Strawberry in the Round

Pattern for jelly jar lid.

Surface Preparation

Sand and seal the wooden lid with Designs From the Heart Wood Sealer. Paint the inside surface with Ceramcoat Ivory. Paint the rim of the lid with Creamcoat Crimson and antique with AC + Blk.

Strawberry

Dark area	CRM + AC + RS
Buff	CRM + YO − CYD + NY
Light area	Buff mix + NYL
Shade	AC + RS + Blk
Highlight	W + CL
Tint	W + Blk

See **Strawberry Step by Step** *for instructions for seeds and depressions on page 74.*

Bract

Base	Blk + CL + W
Shade	Base mix + Blk
Highlight	W + CL − W
Tint	W + Blk

Source

The jelly jars and lids may be ordered from
A Touch of Class by Aileen
11215 Inverness Ct. NE
Albuquerque, NM 87111-7547

Grapes Step by Step

Grapes are fun, exciting and challenging. Many color setups may be used for grapes as they come in a lot of different colors. To build the dimension needed in a large cluster of grapes, there must be sharp contrast in the values. The grapes must be in harmony with the background. Grapes are developed with three different shadows: crescent, modified crescent and triangular. Be aware of these shadows as you paint the grape.

To develop a transparent look in a grape, the strong light will appear in the shadow area and the strong darks appear in the light. A cluster of grapes will create numerous areas of reflected light. However, these reflections cannot appear on the grape where it is touching another grape or surface. These reflected lights help to build the dimension in a cluster of grapes.

1 Grapes are much easier to paint if they are blocked in with an underpainting—using color on top of color or color side by side—and allowed to dry before the strong darks, highlights and reflected lights are glazed on. If using color side by side, block in the dark area in a crescent shape that goes halfway to two-thirds of the way around the grape. This is applied with pressure and is rough and hacky. The buffing color can be applied in just one or two areas, or it can completely surround the crescent, creating a stronger buffing color in the grape. As you apply the buffing color, begin the blending process by blending the dark area and buffing color. Block in the remainder of the grape with the light-area color. Blend between the colors, removing any hard, definite lines. When painting a cluster of grapes, keep in mind the position and value of each grape in the cluster.

2 To glaze over a dry underpainting, apply Winsor & Newton's Blending and Glazing Medium with a clean brush in a thin application, using very little pressure. Load the brush with one of the shading colors and apply with pressure in the darker shadow areas of the crescent. Add a touch of dark in the small stem hole, if there is one. Dry wipe and edge-blend these dark areas into the shadow area. If the shading color is traveling outside the base color, load the brush with that base color and blend back into the shading. Leave the crescent very rough and hacky as this begins to build the feeling of haze on the grape.

3 Apply the highlight with pressure in the area in direct line with the light source. Stack this highlight as many times as necessary to build the appropriate highlight, keeping in mind the position of the grape. Edge-blend the highlight and then soften over the entire area. For a stem area, pull the light around the front of it. Using the chisel edge of the brush, apply the dull, reflected light on the outside edge of the grape. It should be applied in a triangular shape (not a line against a line) with one of the tint colors. Softly blend this into the grape.

4 After the grapes are dry, analyze them. If the darks need to be darker, the midvalue replaced, color cleared or the highlights strengthened, you should glaze the grape again. The final high shine on the more prominent grapes may be glazed or scumbled on. Apply a smaller glint in the reflected light area and just barely soften it out.

Grapes All Around

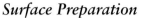

Surface Preparation

Stain the base of the horse with BU alkyd and deepen the edges with BU + Blk. Paint the spindles and the bottom of the legs with Ceramcoat Black acrylic. Apply a light wash of Ceramcoat Lichen Grey to the body of the horse. Antique over this with BU + Blk alkyd paint. Attach the three sections of the pattern by matching the As and Bs. Rouge touches of W + Blk around the completed design, then work touches of AC into the edges of the W + Blk. If necessary, add Winsor & Newton's Blending and Glazing Medium to the paint so it's easier to move. Rub in a circular motion using a soft cloth to remove hard, definite lines. Rouging may be applied several times to give additional depth.

A

Center back

Refer to photo for placement of tendrils.

Blue Grapes

Dark area	PB + Blk
Buff	CRL + YO − (CYD + YO)
Light area	Buff mix + NYL + W
Shade	Dark area mix + Blk
Highlight	NYL + W − W
Tint	W + Blk − W + AC

Blue-Violet Grapes #1

Dark area	PB + DP + Blk
Buff	AC
Light area	Dark area mix + NYL + W
Shade	Dark area mix + Blk + (PB)
Highlight	NYL + W − W
Tint	W + Blk − AC + W

Blue-Violet Grapes #2

Dark area	PB + AC + DP + Blk
Light area	Dark area mix + NYL + W
Shade	Dark area mix + Blk
Highlight	NYL + W − W
Tint	W + Blk − W + OC

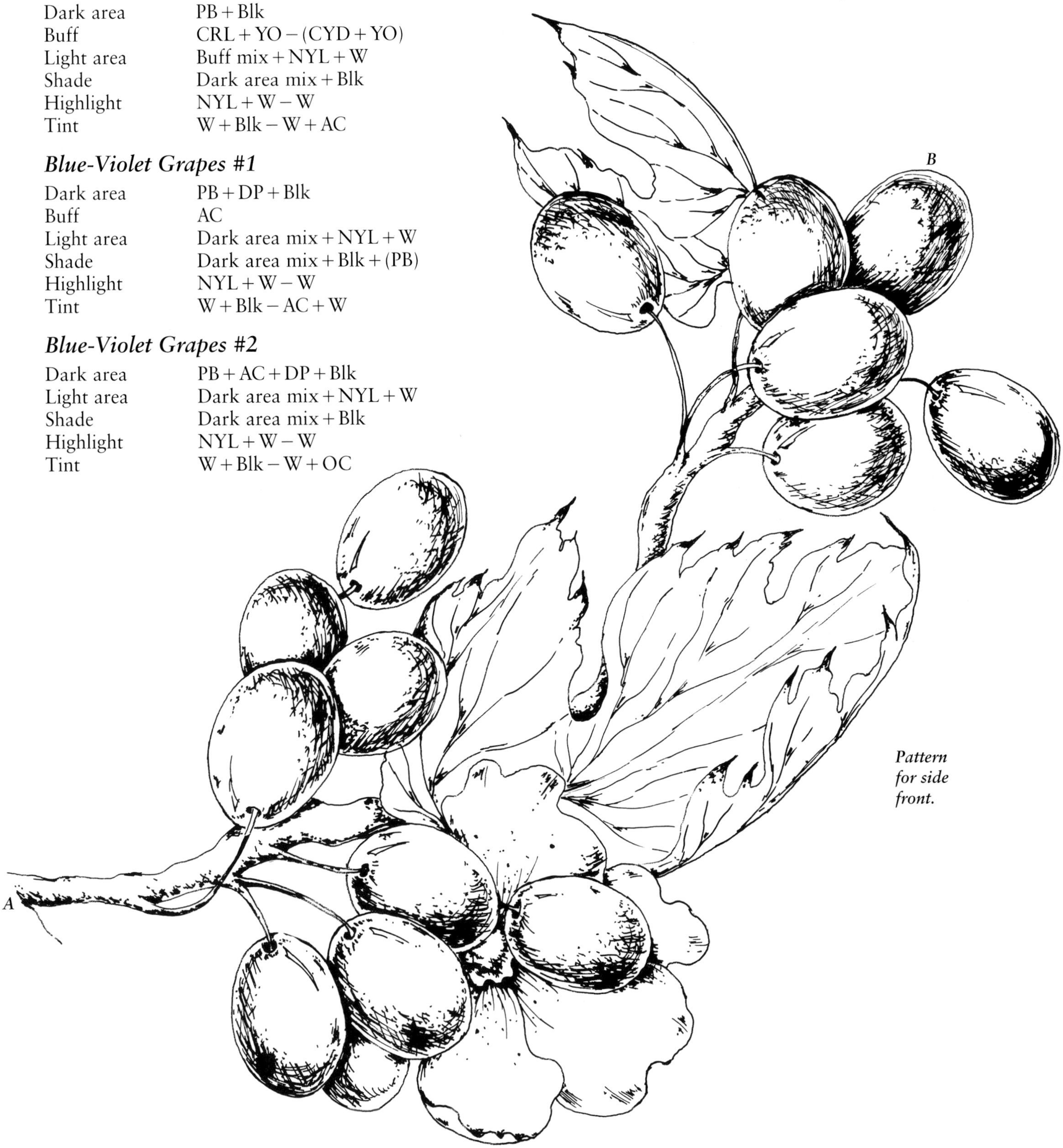

Pattern for side front.

Continued on pages 84-85.

Grapes All Around

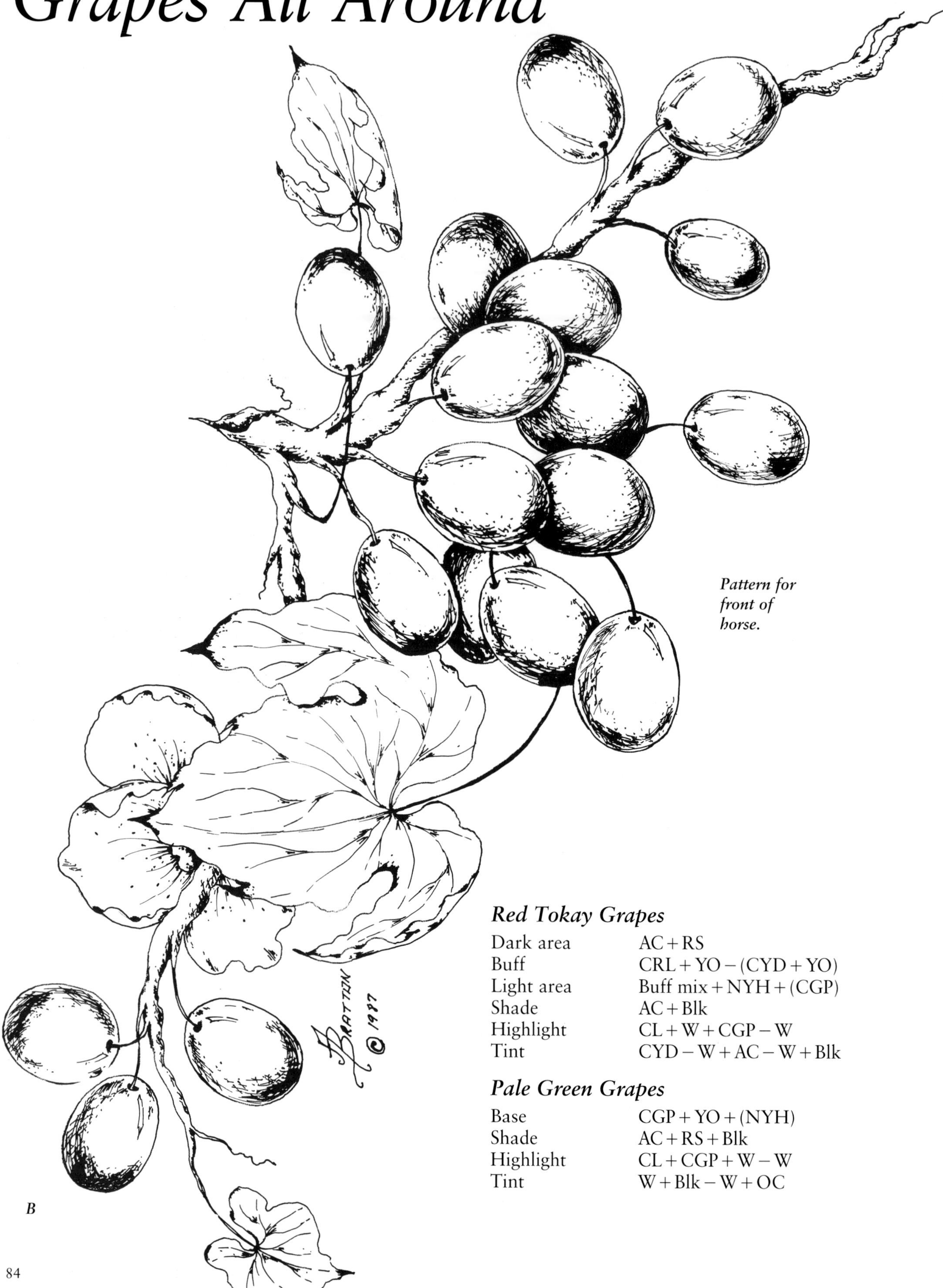

Pattern for front of horse.

B

Red Tokay Grapes

Dark area	AC + RS
Buff	CRL + YO − (CYD + YO)
Light area	Buff mix + NYH + (CGP)
Shade	AC + Blk
Highlight	CL + W + CGP − W
Tint	CYD − W + AC − W + Blk

Pale Green Grapes

Base	CGP + YO + (NYH)
Shade	AC + RS + Blk
Highlight	CL + CGP + W − W
Tint	W + Blk − W + OC

Darker Green Grapes

Dark area   AC + RS + Blk
Buff   CRL + YO
Light area   CGP + CL + W
Shade   AC + Blk
Highlight   CGP + (CL) + W − W
Tint   CYD − W + Blk − W + AC

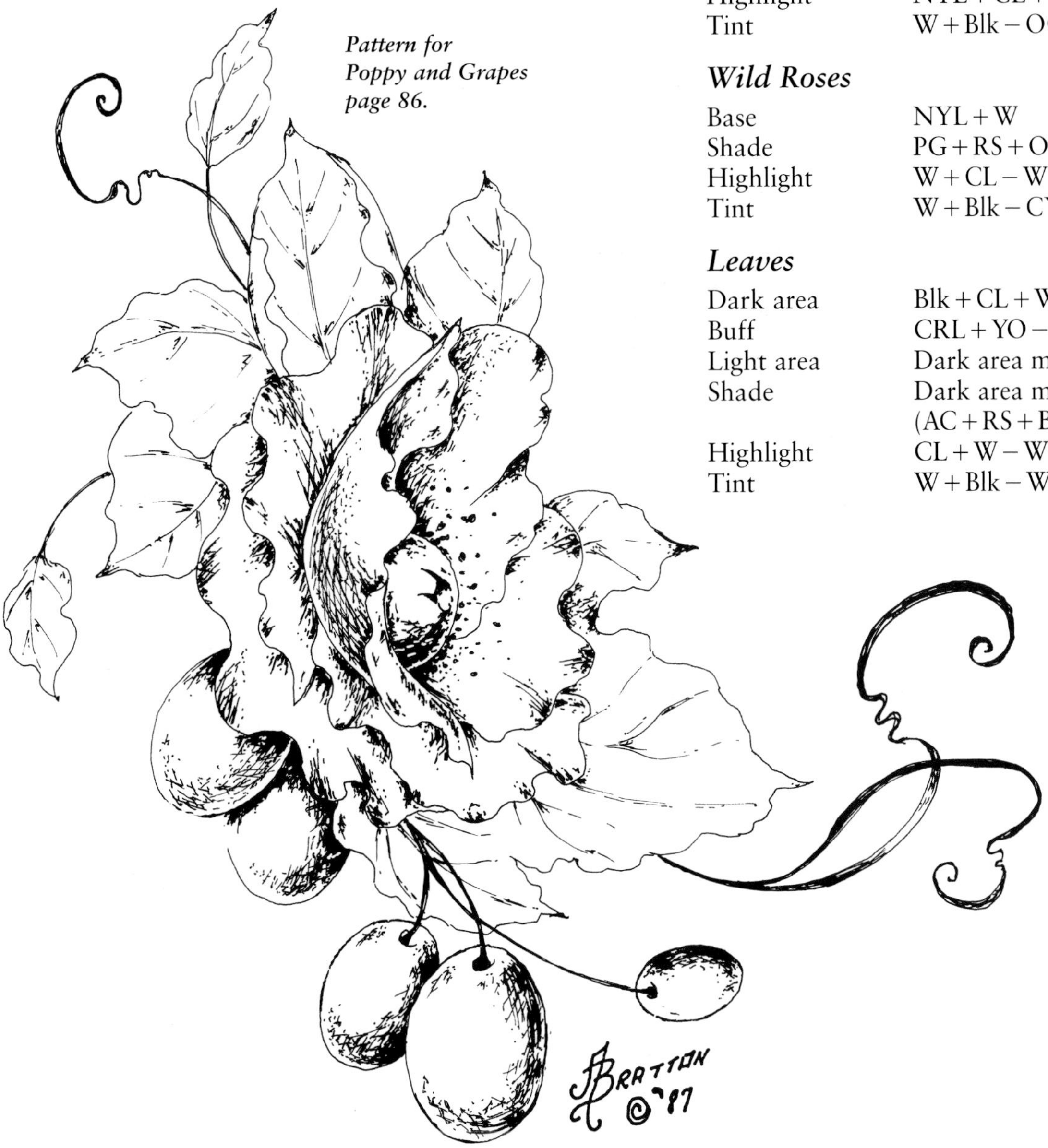

*Pattern for
Poppy and Grapes
page 86.*

Violet Grapes

Dark area   DP + AC + Blk
Buff   AC + RS − (CRL + YO)
Light area   Dark area mix + NYL
Shade   Dark area mix + Blk + (PB)
Highlight   NYL + W − W
Tint   W + Blk − W + AC

Cool Green Grapes

Dark area   PG + OC + Blk
Light area   Dark area mix + NYL + W
Shade   Dark area mix + OC + Blk
Highlight   NYL + CL + W − W
Tint   W + Blk − OC

Wild Roses

Base   NYL + W
Shade   PG + RS + OC
Highlight   W + CL − W
Tint   W + Blk − CYM

Leaves

Dark area   Blk + CL + W − (CGP)
Buff   CRL + YO − YO − RS − CYD
Light area   Dark area mix + CL + (CGP) + W
Shade   Dark area mix + Blk − (PB) −
               (AC + RS + Blk)
Highlight   CL + W − W − (CGP)
Tint   W + Blk − W + OC

Poppy and Grapes

Surface Preparation

Apply an opaque covering or a light wash of Ceramcoat Normandy Rose. This design would also work nicely on a wash of Ceramcoat Ivory. Antique the edges with DP + AC + NYH + Blk. Spatter with this same mixture. Apply the final application of varnish before gluing the lace to the back of the heart.

Poppy

Dark area	AC + DP + NY
Light area	NYH + NYL
Shade	AC + DP + NYH + (Blk)
Highlight	W + CL − W
Accent	CRL

Center

Base	Blk
Highlight	W
Shade	Blk + (PB)
Splotches	W + Blk − W

Leaves

Base	CL + Blk + (W)
Shade	Base mix + Blk
Highlight	W + CL − W
Tint	W + Blk

Grapes

Dark area	AC + DP + NYH + (Blk)
Light area	CGP + NY
Shade	AC + DP + NYH + Blk
Highlight	NYL + W − W − CGP + W − W
Accent	CRL

Poppy Step by Step

A poppy is a very simple flower to paint when the petals lay flat—the difficulty increases when flips, folds, ruffles and pleats are added. Poppies are very light and fragile flowers with delicate, transparent petals. They can be developed using color side by side or color on top of color, depending upon the desired final results. The center can be kept very soft and light, or it can be very dramatic with sharp contrast and detail. Review the section on flips, ruffles, pleats and folds on pages 52-54 to execute these properly.

1 Brush-mix the dark-area values and apply on each petal with pressure, leaving the outside edge very rough and hacky. As the dark is placed around an area, try to keep from outlining it by letting up on the pressure in some areas connecting the darker areas when you are blending the colors or applying the buffing colors.

2 If a buffing color is used it would be applied next. Sometimes the buffing color will touch the entire dark area. If the middle value is strong, develop the poppy in this manner. At other times the buffing color may only touch the dark area in several small areas. When applying the buffing color, pull into the dark area with short, choppy strokes, starting the blending process.

3 The light area is applied to the remainder of the poppy and is pulled into the buffing or dark areas as it is applied. Pressure the colors together by working between them, being careful to remove hard, definite lines but keeping the colors in the areas where they were placed. When finished with these steps, if using oils, the paint should be thin enough that the background is peeking through. If using alkyds, the application of paint should be heavier and more opaque.

4 Apply the shading in the shadow areas to develop depth, flips, ruffles, folds and pleats. When applying the shading, do so with pressure, avoiding outlining an area. Edge-blend by just blending the outside region of the shadow area. Evaluate your shadow areas. If the second-value darks are not dark enough, apply them once again.

5 Highlights will be stacked. The first highlight will be one value lighter than the base mixture. The highlight is applied with pressure and pulled out onto the petals. Build the highlights to be as strong as needed to develop the petals. Each highlight gets lighter in value and smaller in area. Place your brush half on the outside edge of the highlight, blending this into the base with short, cross-

hatching strokes. Dry wipe often and lightly blend over the remaining portion of the petal. If the highlights need to be strengthened, apply them once again in the more prominent areas.

6 Evaluate your painting, keeping in mind the placement of the subject in the design and its relationship to the background. To appear to have shape, form and dimension, the petal must have dark, middle and light values. Each one of these values should contain several value changes. Add tints at this time.

Center

1 To develop the dramatic center of a poppy, think of a baseball cap with sections radiating out from the center button. Block in a dome shape with no flat areas, using very dry black paint.

2 Take a stylus or the wooden end of your brush and pull out paint in the "button" area. If the poppy is tilted so

Continued on page 89.

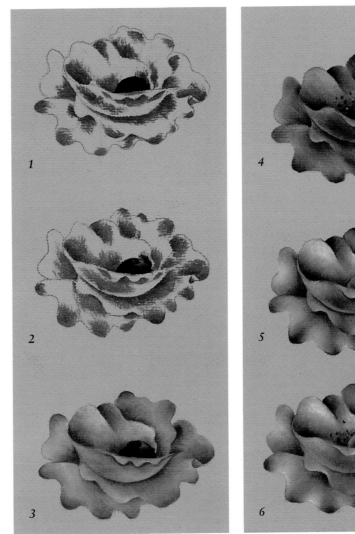

1

2

3

4

5

6

It's Poppy Time

Surface Preparation

Remove the clock face from the clock. (There are small screws in the back.) Sand and seal with Designs From the Heart Wood Sealer. Paint the front of the clock with Ceramcoat Ivory. Paint the side of the clock with Ceramcoat Medium Flesh. Be careful none of the peach color gets on the front of the clock. Spray lightly with Krylon Matte #1311 before lightly applying the pattern.

Before beginning the painting, build the rouging effect: using a flat brush, apply W + Blk mixed with a touch of Winsor & Newton's Blending and Glazing Medium around the poppies, strawberry and leaves at the base of the clock. Pull some of this mixture out further at some points. Work touches of YO into the W + Blk mixtures in a few areas. Let this set for just a few minutes, then, using a soft cloth in a circular motion, rub the edge of the rouging out into the background. Don't overdo the rouging before painting the design, but when the design is complete and several coats of Krylon Matte #1311 have been applied to protect the painting, the rouging may be deepened and reinforced. Repeating the rouging several times gives your background more depth.

Light Poppy

Dark area	AC + RS + CRL
Buff	CRL + NYH
Light area	NYL
Shade	AC + RS + (Blk)
Highlight	CL + NYL + W − W
Tint	W + Blk

Dark Poppy

Base	AC + RS + CRL
Shade	AC + Blk
Highlight	CL + NYL + W − W
Tint	W + Blk

Poppy Center

Base	Blk
Shade	Blk + (PB)
Highlight	W
Tint	W + Blk
Splotches	Blk − W + Blk

Leaves

Base	PG + CL + W
Shade	Base mix + Blk + (PB)
Highlight	CL + W – W
Tint	W + Blk

Dark-Value Strawberries

Dark area	AC + CRL + RS
Light area	NYH + CRL + NYR
Shade	Dark area mix + Blk
Highlight	NYL + W
Tint	W + Blk

Middle-Value Strawberries

Dark area	CRL + AC + RS
Light area	NYR + NYL
Shade	Dark area mix + AC + (Blk)
Highlight	NYL + W – W
Tint	W + Blk

Light-Value Strawberries

Base	NYR + NYL
Shade	CRL + AC
Highlight	W
Tint	W + Blk

Seeds

Depression	AC + CRL + RS
Seed	CRL + NYH
Texture	W

Poppy Step by Step

Continued from page 87.

more petals show in front than in back, the button should be placed very close to the back edge of the center. Study how light hits the opening of a round container to paint the center: The strongest light hits on the outside area of the button directly in line with the light source, and the strongest dark hits on the inside next to the light. Opposite the strong dark is a dull light. On the outside of the dull light is a dull dark. Use a small, flat brush to apply the white highlight with pressure in front of the button area. Place what color is left in the brush on the inside of the button area where the dull light hits. The larger the highlight is, the fuller the center will be, so let it taper down. Softly blend. Reinforce the black base with more Blk in the shadow area. If the Blk isn't dark enough, pick up a tad of PB to deepen.

3 Place a dull, reflected light on the outside edge of the center with W + Blk and softly blend onto the center.

4 Using either the chisel edge of a small flat brush or a round brush, pull down curved lines (if these are straight, the center will appear flat) resembling the sections of a cap. They are triangular as they leave the button area, tapering to very fine lines at the base of the center. Splotches are applied first with Blk then some with W + Blk. These are applied with the corner of a flat brush or a round brush. Some splotches should be large and some small. Be sure not to make dots. Let several fall farther away from the center so as not to create a ring. If a front petal comes up over the base of the center, splotches will only be seen on the back and perhaps the side petals.

For a Less Dramatic Center:

1 Block in the center, keeping a rounded shape at the top. Shade along the base and pull up a crescent shape as indicated by the light source. Blend into the base.

2 Apply a highlight that falls in line with the source of light. Stack the highlights and blend. Apply splotches as described above, using the shading color and highlight colors.

It's Poppy Time

Poppin' Peaches

Pattern on pages 92-94, instructions on page 95.

Peach Step by Step

1 Load the brush with the dark area mix (YO + CYD) and place down the upper left quadrangle under the leaf and pull out the lower crescent shape. Place this dark area mix also in the area to the right of the plunge line. With the paint left in the brush, pull some dark to the left of the plunge line. Dry wipe and load the brush with the buffing mix and completely surround the dark area. Blend the two areas as you apply the buffing. Dry wipe brush and load with the light area mix (NYL + CL + W) and apply to the remainder of the peach. Blend the light area into the buffing area. Lightly soften over the entire peach.

2 Load the brush with the shading color (CRL + RS). Place shading within the original dark area. To blend, place the edge of the brush half on the shading and half on the base and softly pull the two color edges together. Deepen the lower area of the crescent as well as one small area to the left of the plunge line with the shading color (AC + RS). Softly blend the outside edge of this color into the other shading area.

Step 1

Step 2

Pattern for Poppin Peaches *side of box.*

Step 3

Step 4

3 Load the brush with the highlight color (W + CL). Applying with pressure, stack a smaller, lighter highlight on top and then a pure white one on top of that. Edge-blend the outside edge of the first highlight into the base of the peach. Dry wipe the brush often and soften over the entire highlight.

4 Place the tint (W + Blk) just under the leaf on the left side. Also place one on the right edge, pulling into the dark area as illustrated. If the tint appears muddy, it is too dark. Pick up more W and apply over the top. Blend with soft, choppy strokes, giving a rough and fuzzy feeling to the peach.

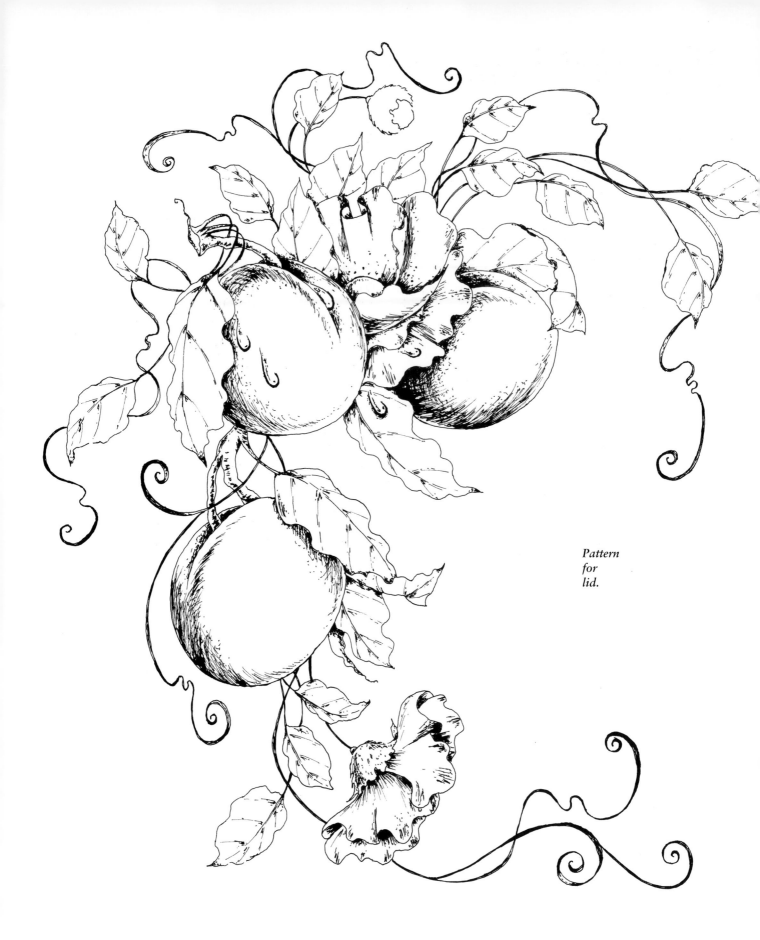

*Pattern
for
lid.*

Poppin' Peaches

Continued from pages 92-93.

Surface Preparation

Stain the side of the lid and handle with BU alkyd. Paint the lid with a light wash of Ceramcoat Medium Flesh. Deepen the antiquing on the edge with BU + AC + CRL, softly pulling the color out onto the top of the box and softening it into the background. Paint the bottom of the box and the top portion of the inside with Americana Georgia Clay. Paint the inside rim of the lid with Ceramcoat Medium Flesh and the flat surface with Americana Georgia Clay. Line the box with a pretty coordinating fabric. After the design is painted, spatter the lid with BU + AC + CRL. Spatter the bottom with CRL + NYH + W.

Light-Value Peach

Dark area	YO + CYD
Buff	Dark area mix + NYH + NYL
Light area	NYL + CL + W
Shade	CRL + RS − AC + RS
Highlight	W + CL − W
Tint	W + Blk

Middle-Value Peach

Dark area	CRL + CYD + RS
Buff	CYD + YO
Light area	Buff mix + NYH + NYL
Shade	CRL + AC + RS + (BU)
Highlight	CL + NYL + (W) − W
Tint	W + Blk − CRL + YO

Dark-Value Peach

Dark area	CRL + RS
Buff	CYD + YO
Light area	Buff mix + NYH
Shade	CRL + AC + RS − AC + BU
Highlight	NYL + CL + W − NYL
Tint	W + Blk-CYD + YO

Poppies

Dark area	AC + RS
Buff	CRL + YO
Light area	Buff mix + NYH + NYL
Shade	AC + BU
Highlight	NYL + CL + W − W
Tint	W + Blk

Poppy Center

Base	NYH
Shade	AC + RS + BU
Highlight	W + CL − W
Tint	W + Blk
Splotches	Blk − Blk + W

Leaves

Base	PG + CL + W + (Blk)
Shade	Base mix + Blk + (PB)
Highlight	W + CL − W
Tint	RS − YO − CRL + AC + RS − W + Blk

Rose Step by Step

1 Fluff in the dark area with a large, flat brush. Place the dark color inside the bowl and under the bowl and the remainder of the lower petals from about three o'clock to nine o'clock. Place a small amount of the same color on the lower part of the bowl, leaving a narrow area void of color between the two dark areas. Dry wipe your brush and load it with the light area fluff and apply to the remainder of the rose. Soften the areas between the two colors by blending with short, choppy strokes.

2 Paint the back petals of the bowl first. Load the short end of the brush with pressure, using ample paint but not so much that you will leave ridges. The first color on the outside edge of the brush should be close to the same value as your background and the intensity should be dull. The first petal should start at about eleven o'clock, arch at twelve o'clock and end about one o'clock. Lift your brush and reload. Start the next stroke at one o'clock, leaving a small, V-shaped gap between the two strokes. This stroke should arch at two o'clock and end at three. As you come to three o'clock, come up on the chisel edge and pull down so it will point toward six o'clock. Turn your painting so you can start the third stroke at eleven o'clock, leaving a small gap between petals. You should push out on the brush so the petal is rounded at about ten o'clock. You are creating the illusion of many rows of petals. To be soft, they do not need to be definite. The back section of the bowl usually has three rows of petals, dropping down about an ⅛ inch each time. Keep the arch at twelve o'clock—don't allow the petals to become straight or flat across the top. The color should become lighter in value as you come forward. Sometimes it is nice to tint the top edge of a back petal. To keep the bottom edge of the petals of the last row soft, keep the pressure on the top edge of the brush. Remember, each row of the back section of the bowl is a duplication of the first row in shape.

3 Start the petals for the front of the bowl by loading the brush with a light value on the longer bristles and a dark value on the short bristles. Remember as you come forward, each row should get lighter in value. You can create a tight rose by keeping the chisel edges of the side of each stroke of the bowl close, or you can make it more open by leaving more space between them. The top edge of the first bowl should be slightly below an imaginary line drawn from three o'clock to nine o'clock. To start the stroke, place the brush on the chisel edge just above the imaginary line between three and nine o'clock. Angle the brush between ten and eleven o'clock and pull down and towards the middle, making a semicircle. Avoid a square look. If you find it difficult to end the petal in the same way you started, try making two halves in the same manner and allowing the strokes to meet in the center. The chisel edge of the bowl stroke, on the right, ends above three o'clock and is angled between one and two o'clock. It isn't necessary to connect each petal to the chisel edge of a back petal. Drop each bowl only an ⅛ inch or less. Leaving an opening in the petal in the front row is sometimes desirable, but don't make it in the center of the rose. The back petals and the front of the bowl should comprise approximately two-thirds of the rose.

Continued on page 98.

Tips for Painting Beautiful Roses

The stroke rose has always been the ultimate in decorative painting to me and I love to paint and teach them. Read the following tips carefully, as they will help you succeed at painting the stroke rose of your dreams.

I teach the rose using the positions on the clock to describe the position of each stroke. To do so, we must define where twelve o'clock is on the rose. Think of the rose as a round object (slightly extended to an oval shape), divided into three sections. The top of the rose, or bowl, has a back section (the first section to be painted) and a front section (the second section to be painted). The third section to be painted is the bottom petals. The furthermost petals of the back section are arched the highest at twelve o'clock. This is the top, center of the back section. The bottom of the last stroke in the third section should rest at the six o'clock point. The rose is widest at three and nine o'clock.

The rose is painted with an angle brush. The length of the bristles are very important: If they are too long, it is difficult to control the strokes and the brush will spread out, making the petal too wide. Most of the angle brushes on the market are too long, or the bristles are made of a synthetic mixture that isn't resilient enough to bounce back properly. I recommend Winsor & Newton's series 760 in the ⅛-inch, ¼-inch, ½-inch and ⅜-inch sizes.

What happens on the palette and the technique used to load the brush are very important. Place your colors on the palette with the darkest color in the upper right corner, moving across the top according to values. Leave an adequate space to the right and left of each color to develop paths of color when loading the brush. This is done by plac-ing the short end of an angle brush just a tad into the dark color and pulling down the side of each strip of color on both sides. After each of the dark values are loaded on the brush, load the long end of the brush by pulling down each side of the light-value strip. The area created on each side of the color is the path of color. If you make a mistake when creating these paths, pick the color up with your palette knife and move it to a new area of your palette. If the path of color doesn't have a nice blend of dark, medium and light values, start a new one.

When transferring the rose pattern, apply only the outside edges, the top edge and the bottom of the bowl. Use a fluff of color for the base color, allowing some of the background to show through. One of the keys to painting a stroke rose is applying enough pressure on the upper edge of the brush (the longer bristles). If the proper pressure is applied, you maintain control and create clean lines. If you double load the brush, the dark color helps to build the contrast and depth in the rose. You may come back and add stronger darks later, as discussed in step 5, but double-loading the brush will help eliminate this need. Remember that the light color (the long end of the bristles) is always on the outside edge of the rose and the dark color (short end of the bristles) is always on the inside of the petal or rose. When double loading, apply pressure so the colors blend together and no hard, definite line appears between colors. Using a palette made up of at least half alkyds makes painting the rose easier because the alkyd paint has more body.

4 The outside, bottom petals are painted last and should wrap around each other. The first stroke is a short stroke. Load the brush with a color close to the value of the background and dull in intensity. On the right, the stroke should start at three o'clock and end just past four o'clock, coming up to the edge of the bottom of the bowl on the chisel edge. The stroke on the left starts at nine o'clock and slides in just past eight o'clock. Start the third petal at about four o'clock and slide just past six o'clock, being careful not to end dead center. The fourth stroke starts at eight o'clock and slides past where the third petal ends. The fifth stroke fills the gap between the last two petals.

5 You are now ready to refine the rose. Deepen the inside of the bowl, keeping the darkest color to one side. You may add darks and strengthen highlights to create more dimension and sparkle in your stroke rose. Tints may also be added at this time. The bottom of the rose may require a few additional petals. Some of these may be smaller petals that fit inside the established ones and they may pull out and end beyond the original petals. Slices or slivers of petals indicate just an edge of the petal is visible. These are done with the chisel edge of the brush loaded with a light, bright, intense color. You may place small splotches in the darkest area of the bowl with a small liner brush, using the lightest and darkest values in the rose. You can thin the paint with Winsor & Newton's Blending and Glazing Medium to create a softer look.

Pattern for top of Springtime Bath Boutique, pages 100-103.

Step 1

Step 2

Step 5

Step 3

Step 4

Springtime Bath Boutique

Springtime Bath Boutique

Surface Preparation

Sand and seal the surface with Designs From the Heart Wood Sealer. Paint the surface with Ceramcoat Ivory. Mist lightly with Krylon Matte #1311 and lightly apply the pattern. Refer to page 8 for instructions on applying gold leaf over Red Iron Oxide acrylic on the edges of the project, the top of the hand lotion dispenser and on the entire soap dish. Lightly antique the gold leafing with BU. When the design is dry, rub W + Blk and touches of YO in and around the designs on all objects. Spatter with various mixtures from the light green leaf. For a nice touch to complement this set, paint roses or violets on decorative guest soaps—you can even spray the painted soaps lightly with Krylon Matte #1311 for protection, or use a waterbase varnish such as Right Step.

Remainder of pattern on page 98.

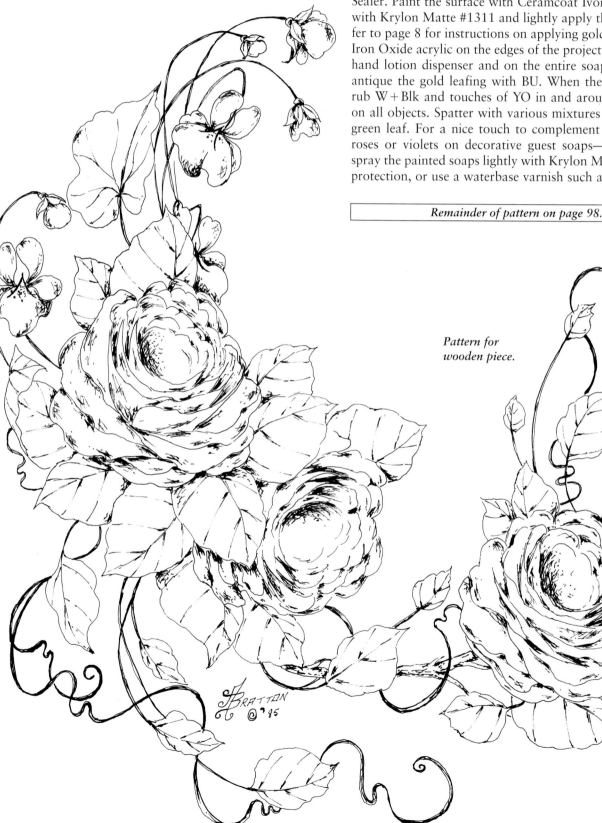

Pattern for wooden piece.

Light-Value Mauve Roses

Dark fluff	AC + DP + RS + NYH
Light fluff	NYR + NYL + W

Overstroke
Load the short end of the brush with AC, DP, RS and then Blk (optional). Load the long end of the brush with NYR, NYL and W.

Tint	W + Blk − CRL − CYD

Medium-Value Mauve Roses

Dark fluff	AC + DP + RS + NYH
Light fluff	NYR + NYL + CRL + (NYR)

Overstroke
Load the short end of the brush with AC, DP, RS, NYH and Blk (optional). Load the long end of the brush with CRL (optional), NYH, NYR and NYL.

Tint	CRL

Pink Rose

Dark fluff	AC + RS + DP + CRL
Light fluff	CRL + CYD + NYH + NYL + W

Overstroke
Load short end of brush with AC, RS, DP, CRL (optional) and Blk (optional). Load long end of brush with NYR, NYL, BYL and W.

Tint	CRL + CYD

Leaves

Dark area	PG + CL + W
Buff	YO − RS
Light area	Dark area mix + CL + W
Shade	Dark area mix + Blk + (PB)
Highlight	W + CL − W
Tint	W + Blk − DP + RS + AC

Accent Leaves

Dark area	DP + AC + RS
Buff	CL
Light area	W + CL
Shade	Dark area mix + Blk
Highlight	W + CL − W
Tint	W + Blk

*Pattern
for lotion
dispenser.*

Light-Value Violets

Base	NYR + NYL
Shade	AC + DP + NYH
Highlight	W + CL − W
Tint	W + Blk

Middle-Value Violets

Dark area	NYR + AC + DP + RS
Light area	NYR + NYL
Shade	Dark area mix + Blk
Highlight	NYR + NYL + W
Tint	W + Blk

Dark-Value Violets

Base	DP + AC + RS + Blk
Highlight	NYH − NYR + NYL
Shade	DP + AC + Blk
Tint	W + Blk
Dark lines	DP + AC + Blk
Splotches	CL + W

 Source

All surfaces in this project may be ordered from
A Touch of Class by Aileen
11215 Inverness Ct. NE
Albuquerque, NM 87111-7547

Lily Step by Step

Step 1

Step 2

Step 3

1 Block in the dark area (Blk + CL + W) of the heart-shaped petals. Buff the dark area with CL. Blend the two areas with short, choppy strokes. Block in the remainder of the petal with the light area mix (W + YO). Begin to connect the colors by pulling one color into the other with short, choppy strokes. Soften over the entire petal. Block in the remaining three petals with W + YO. Apply the shading color of Blk + CL + W to all the petals. Blend the shading out with short, choppy strokes.

2 Apply the highlights of W + CL − W to build dimension, depth and form in the petals. Stack the strong highlights at least three times.

3 Blend highlights with short, choppy strokes, softening the outside edge of the first highlight. Dry wipe the brush often. Continue to blend the outside edges of the highlights until blended. Soften over the entire petal. Add tints of CRL + R + W + CRD (optional) to all the petals as illustrated. Softly edge-blend these colors into the base. Refine the petal by blending in the growth direction. Add stronger W to the center of the center vein area. With a liner brush and CRD + AC + Blk thinned with Winsor & Newton's Blending and Glazing Medium, apply the lines on the center petals. Add the medium to Blk + CL + W and add the stamen.

Classy Keepsakes

Classy Keepsakes

These boxes are so lovely and make such neat boxes for all our precious keepsakes. They make lovely gifts and look attractive individually or in a grouping. I've used Peruvian lilies in this design. I received a bouquet containing these flowers and fell in love with this particular kind of lily. They are a little different from the ordinary lily as they are smaller, and the three side petals are more heart-shaped.

Surface Preparation

Frost the glass tops of the boxes as described on page 8. Tape the line drawing of the pattern to the inside of the lid and you're ready to begin your painting.

Pink Blossoms

Dark area	CRD + CRL + RS
Buff	Dark area mix + CRL + YO
Light area	Buff mix + YO + W
Shade	CRD + AC + Blk
Highlight	W + CL − W
Tint	W + Blk

Blossom Center

Base	YO
Shade	AC + RS + (Blk)
Highlight	W + CL − W
Lines and splotches	AC + CRD + Blk

Back Center Lily Petals

Dark area	Blk + CL + W
Buff	CL
Light area	W + YO
Shade	Blk + CL + W
Highlight	W + CL − W
Tint	CRL + RS + W + (CRD)

Other Lily Petals

Base	W + YO
Shade	Blk + CL + W
Highlight	W + CL − W
Tint	CRL + RS + W + (CRD)
Lines on center petal	CRD + AC + Blk
Stamen	Blk + CL + W

Leaves #1

Dark area	Blk + CL + W
Buff	YO
Light area	Dark area mix + CL + W
Shade	Dark area mix + Blk + (PB)
Highlight	W + CL − W
Tint	W + Blk

Leaves #2

Dark area	VG + Blk + CL
Buff	YO
Light area	Dark area mix + CL + W
Shade	Dark area mix + Blk
Highlight	W + CL − W
Tint	W + Blk

Buds

Base	W + YO
Shade	Blk + CL + W − CRL + AC + RS
Highlight	W + CL
Tint	W + Blk

Lilies and Lace

This design was painted on a porcelain powder box, but it could also be used for jewelry or potpourri. The porcelain surface is lovely to paint on. Try using alkyd paints on porcelain—you'll love it.

Surface Preparation

Spray the porcelain box with a very light coat of Krylon Matte #1311, then apply the pattern very lightly. The antiquing along the outside edge of the box may be done prior to painting the design or after the design is finished. To antique the edge, put Blk + CL + W on the outside edges. Also add touches of YO + Blk + W. Soften the colors into the porcelain background with a soft rag, rubbing in a circular motion on the inside edge of the color. Gold leaf the bottom of the box, the lip and bottom of the lid, following instructions on page 8. When the box is varnished, apply the lace with a hot-glue gun.

Top Lily

Light Yellow Area in Center Petal

Base	NYL
Shade	NYL + CL

Remainder of Center Petal

Base	CRL + NYL
Shade	CRL + AC + RS
Highlight	NYL + W
Dark lines	AC + RS + (CRL)

Remainder of Top Lily Petals and Other Lily

Dark area	CRL + AC + RS
Light area	Dark area mix + NYL + (NYH)
Shade	AC + RS + Blk
Highlight	NYL + W − W
Tint	W + Blk

Bud

Base	NYL
Shade	Blk + CL + W
Highlight	W + CL + NYL
Tint	CRL + AC + RS − W + Blk

Leaves

Dark area	Blk + CL + W
Light area	Dark area mix + CGP + W
Shade	Dark area mix + Blk
Highlight	CL + CGP + W − W
Tint	W + Blk

Sweet Pea Step by Step

Step 1

Step 2

Step 3

Step 4

1 For the front petals, block in the dark area with AC + CRL. Dry wipe the brush and load it with the buffing color, CYD. Pull the buffing color into the dark area, blending the two areas together as you go. Dry wipe the brush and load with W + CL + YO to block in the remainder of the petal. Blend this color into the buffing area as you apply the light area mix. For the back petal, apply the dark area mix with CL + W as illustrated. Block in the remainder of the petal with NYL. Soften between the two areas, breaking the definite lines.

2 On the front petal, shade as illustrated with AC + RS + Blk (optional). Blend the shading color into the base with short, choppy strokes. Shade the base of the back petal with YO + CL. Dry wipe the brush and blend into the base.

3 On the front petals, place the highlight of W + CL on the ruffled edge, stacking them as needed to bring them forward. Use the same colors on the back petals to develop the ruffles, folds and pleats and to give the petals form and dimension.

4 Blend the outside edge of the highlight with short, choppy strokes, working it into the base. Let up on the pressure and soften over the top of the remaining highlight. On the back petals, add tints of CRL + CYD + YO to the outside ruffled edges. Place this color on, making it heavier in some areas. Soften the bottom edge of the color into the petal. Pick up a deeper value of CRL + AC + RS and place on top of some of the tinted areas. This color should stay on top of the original color and not be blended out beyond the first tint color.

Adeline's Sweet Peas

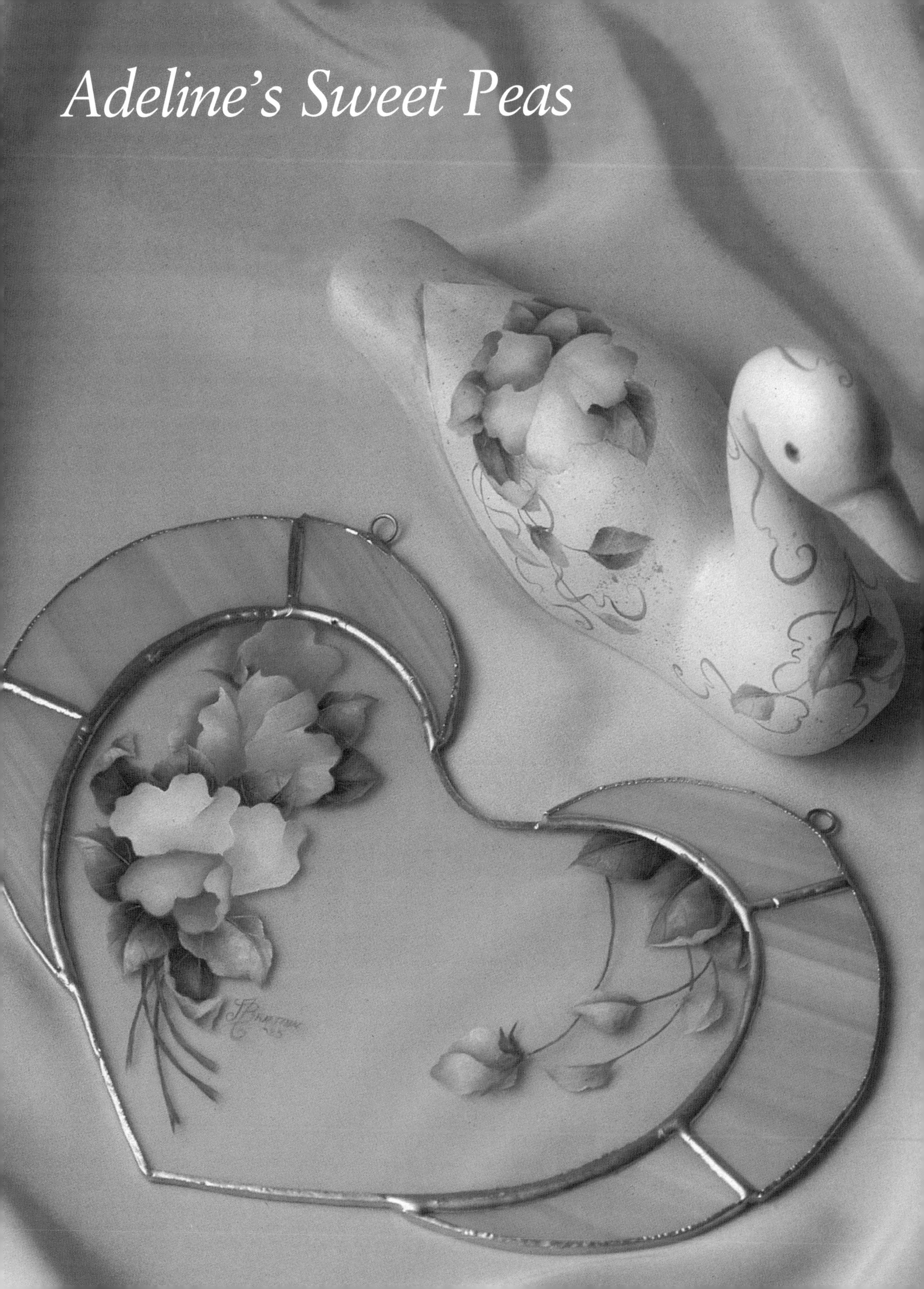

Adeline's Sweet Peas

This stained-glass heart is special, and for that reason I have named it for my mother. I painted sweet peas on it as they are one of my favorite flowers. The little swoose with just a small spray of sweet peas makes a nice accessory for the heart.

Surface Preparation

The glass on the stained-glass heart is frosted as described on page 8. Frequently the stained-glass heart may be purchased with the glass already frosted. To make it easier to paint, I filled the crease down the swoose's back with spackling compound and sanded it until smooth. Seal the swoose with Designs From the Heart Wood Sealer and paint with Ceramcoat Ivory. Paint the tail and beak with Ceramcoat Medium Flesh, then antique and spatter with a mixture of AC + CRL + RS.

Source

The swoose, heart, glass-frosting compound and tool may be ordered from
A Touch of Class by Aileen
11215 Inverness Ct. NE
Albuquerque, NM 87111-7547

*Pattern for
swoose's back.*

Dark-Value Sweet Pea

Base	CRL + AC + (RS)
Shade	AC + RS + (Blk)
Highlight	CL + W − W

Leaves

Dark area	Blk + CL + (W)
Buff	(YO)
Light area	Dark area mix + CL + W
Shade	Dark area mix + Blk + (PB)
Highlight	W + CL − W
Tint	W + Blk

Light-Value Sweet Pea

Front Petals

Dark area	AC + CRL
Buff	CYD
Light area	W + CL + YO
Shade	AC + RS + (Blk)
Highlight	W + CL − W

Back Petals

Dark area	W + CL
Light area	NYL
Shade	YO + CL
Highlight	W + CL − W
Tint edges	CRL + CYD + YO − CRL + AC + RS

Middle-Value Sweet Pea

Front Petals

Dark area	CRL + CYD + (AC)
Light area	CYD + NYL
Shade	AC + CRL + Blk
Highlight	W + CL − W

Back Petals

Dark area	CYM + YO
Buff	CYD + NYL
Light area	CRL + AC + CYD
Shade	CRL + AC + RS
Highlight	CL + W − W

*Pattern for
swoose's chest.*

Magnolia Step by Step

Petals

1 Load your brush with the dark-area mix and apply at the base of the petal, around the center. The dark area will also be placed where a petal falls underneath another petal. These areas are not outlined, but the color should go where the shadow would be the darkest. The dark-area color will also be placed at both ends and in the dip areas of a flip. Dry wipe the brush and load with one of the three buffing colors. Use the darker buffing color (YO) in the deeper, darker shadow areas. Use CGP in the lighter areas closer to the light source. Pull this buffing color into the dark area as you apply it. Not much more blending will be required. Dry wipe the brush and load it with the light area mix (NYL + W) and block in the remainder of the petal. As this color is applied, it should be blended into the buffing area and dark area. Any hard, definite lines between the colors should be broken.

2 Once the petal is blended, it's time to deepen the shadow areas with the shading color. Deepen the darker triangular shadow areas with this mixture and don't let it pull out further than the first dark area. If the dark area is pulled out from the base, it will help to create a scooped-down feeling on the petal. Magnolia petals definitely scoop down toward the center and the tips curve up toward the center.

3 After the shading has been applied and softened into the dark areas, it's time to begin the highlight. W + CL should be applied with pressure and stacked several times on the petals, which are in a direct line from the light source. Highlights should also be placed on the flips as illustrated. Begin to blend the outside edge of the first highlight, softening this into the base color of the petal. Once this has been accomplished, begin to blend over the remaining highlight, softening the color. When the highlights are built to the appropriate level for the position of the petals, begin to add the tints to the petals. The tints of CO − W + Blk − BM should be added as illustrated. Soften over the entire petal to refine it.

Center

1 Block in the center with NYL + W.

2 Apply the shading color (CGP + Blk) just at the base of the center. Softly blend this into the base. Apply the shading color (BM + RS) all along the outside edge of the center and softly blend this into the center.

3 Apply the highlight (W + CL), stacking it several times. Dry wipe the brush and blend the outside edge of the highlight, and then soften over the entire center. The center may dry before adding the detail; however, if the detailing is done while the center is wet, it will really look much nicer. The detail may be glazed on using Winsor & Newton's Blending and Glazing Medium or paint thinner. These lines must be curved or the center will appear flat.

Step 1

Step 2

Step 3

Southern Charm

Southern Charm

I have always been intrigued with magnolia blossoms, as they are one of the flowers I can remember from my childhood: My grandparents had a magnolia tree in their front yard and I thought they were so pretty. This piece looks very nice in an entry way or foyer.

Surface Preparation

Sand, seal and paint the surface with Designs From the Heart Wood Sealer. Paint the surface with Ceramcoat Lichen Grey. Paint the edges of the surface with Liquitex Red Iron Oxide acrylic, gold leaf over this and then antique them with BU. Refer to page 8 for instructions on gold leafing. This project would also look very nice with silver leaf over Red Iron Oxide, again antiqued with BU. When the painting was completed, I rouged W + Blk and touches of YO in several areas. If the colors are hard to fade into the background, use a soft rag, rubbing the edge of the paint in a circular motion.

Light-Value Leaves

Dark area	PB + CO + YO + CL + W
Buff	NYH
Light area	Dark area mix + CL + W
Shade	Dark area mix + Blk
Highlight	CL + W − W
Tint	W + Blk

Medium-Value Leaves

Dark area	PB + CO + YO
Buff	YO
Light area	Dark area mix + CL + W
Shade	Dark area mix + Blk + (PB)
Highlight	NYH + CL + W
Tint	W + Blk

Dark-Value Leaves

Base	PB + CO
Shade	Dark area mix + Blk + (PB)
Highlight	YO + CL + W
Tint	W + Blk

Flips and Underside of Leaves

Dark area	RS + Blk
Buff	YO
Light area	NYH
Shade	Dark area mix + Blk
Highlight	NYH + W

 Source

Mirror may be ordered from
A Touch of Class by Aileen
11215 Inverness Ct. NE
Albuquerque, NM 87111-7547

Magnolia Blossoms

Dark area	RS + CGP + (Blk)
Buff	CGP − YO − NYH
Light area	NYL + W
Highlight	W + CL − W
Shade	RS + Blk + (CGP)
Tint	CO − Blk + W − BM

Magnolia Center

Base	NYL + W
Shade bottom	CGP + Blk
Shade sides	BM + RS
Highlight	W + CL
Tint	W + Blk
Detail	BM + RS

Blackberry and Morning Glory Step by Step

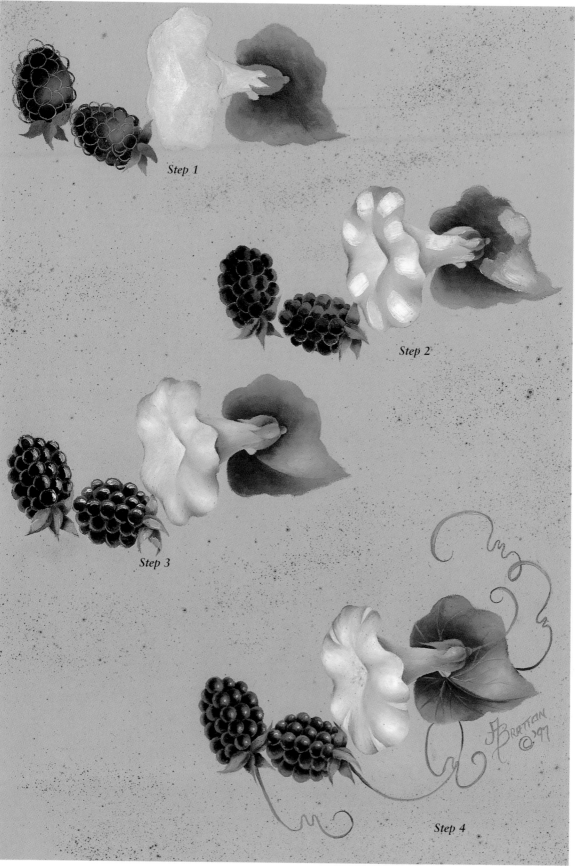

Step 1

Step 2

Step 3

Step 4

Blackberry Delight

Blackberries

1 When making your tracing of the pattern, trace a smaller perimeter for the berry. Block in each blackberry with a different mixture of the base color (PB + Blk + DP + AC). If necessary, apply a deeper value of the mixture to the lower crescent area of each berry and to the area at the top of the berry under each calyx. Apply a highlight to each berry with NYL + W and soften into the berry. The large berry should have shape and dimension. To apply the small berries on the large berry, each one will have to be shaded and highlighted. To position each berry, draw five rows with a stylus. The center row is a full row and each individual berry sits on top of the next. The berries in the two rows on either side of the center do not line up with the center row.

2 Outline each berry with NYL + W, thinned with a medium. Shade each individual berry with a darker value of the mixture used to block it in. As you soften these areas into each berry, do not lose the outside edge of the berry. Using NYL + W, apply a highlight to each individual berry on the center row and the two rows on the side of the center that fall in the direct line of light.

3 Blend these highlights, being careful not to lose each individual berry. Using W + PB, apply a dull, reflected light on the lower side of each berry in the center row and also to the berries in the other two rows that are not in the direct line of light.

4 Let the berries dry and apply the dark shading, the highlight or glint and the cool, dull reflected light, using Winsor & Newton's Blending and Glazing Medium. These areas may need to be glazed several times, letting the berries dry between each application of glaze. The final glints of the highlight and the dull reflected lights may be left very strong.

Morning Glory

1 Block in the morning glory with NYL + W, leaving thin lines unpainted to divide the flips, folds and trumpets of the morning glory.

2 Apply the shading color (W + Blk + WG) as illustrated and blend into the base color. Apply the highlights as illustrated, stacking the most prominent areas.

3 Blend the outside edge of the first highlight into the base, then soften over the top of the remaining highlight until it is blended, working in the growth direction of the flower.

4 Place the triangular white veins on the front of the morning glory with W. Add tints of KB and YO in the midvalue area and next to the triangular white veins.

Blackberry Delight

Blackberry Delight has always been a favorite piece and I wanted to share it with all of you. I hope you will enjoy it.

Surface Preparation

Sand and seal the surface with Designs From the Heart Wood Sealer. Basecoat the surface with Ceramcoat Tide Pool Blue.

Paint the edge of the board with Ceramcoat Light Ivory. Lightly mist the board with Krylon Matte #1311. After the design is finished and has been sprayed with a light coat of Krylon Matte #1311, spatter the edges and surface with a mixture of W + Blk + KB.

Leaves #1

Dark area	Blk + YO
Buff	NYL + CL
Light area	W + CL
Shade	Dark area mix + Blk
Highlight	W + (CL) − W
Tint	W + Blk

Leaves #2

Dark area	Blk + (PB) + CGP
Buff	YO
Light area	W + CL
Shade	Blk + PB
Highlight	W + CL
Tint	W + Blk

Leaves #3

Base	Blk + (PB) + CL + (CGP)
Shade	Base mix + Blk
Highlight	W + Blk

Morning Glories

Base	NYL + W
Shade	Blk + W + (WG)
Highlight	W + NYL + (CL) − W
Tint	KB − YO

Blackberries

Base	Mixtures of Blk + PB + DP + AC
Shade	Blk + PB + DP + (AC)
Highlight	W + NYL − W
Tint	W + PB

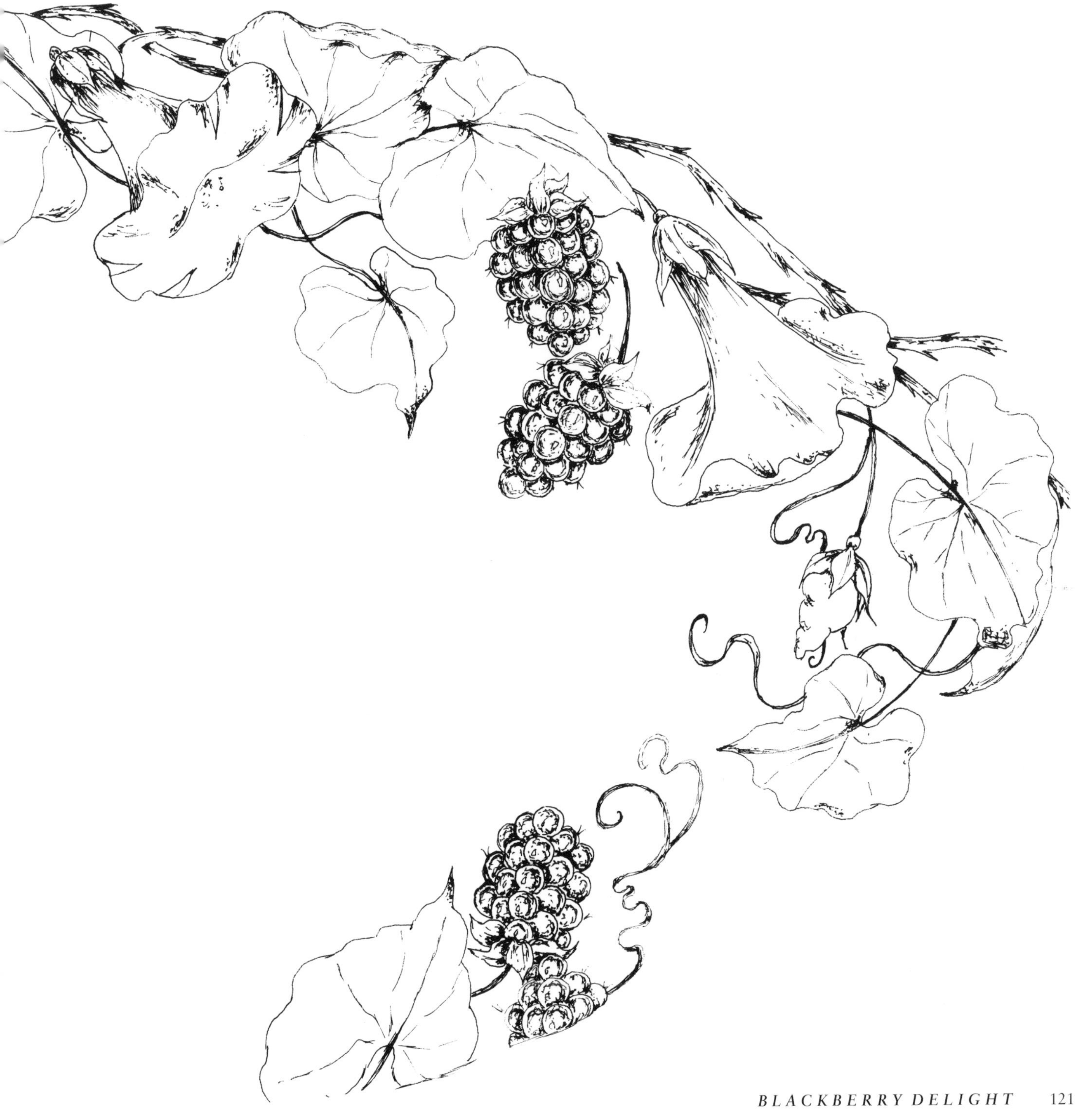

Memories From Yesteryear

Aileen Bratton's Decorative Painting Treasures

Still Life

Webster's Dictionary defines a still life as a representation of inanimate objects. The still life lends itself to being highly individualized. You can create a still-life environment using either real or imaginary objects. The possibilities are endless. Any item can find its place in a still life. In choosing and arranging objects, you can focus on shape and color, or you can select objects based on their emotional or symbolic significance. The still life offers freedom of expression in many ways.

I have saved this still life for last as it is more advanced than most of the other projects in this book, with its combination of fruit, flowers, containers, drapery and cast shadows. Sharply focused still-life paintings require neatness, attention to detail and patience. It is best to paint this still life in stages.

Tips for Successfully Applying a Still-Life Design

1 Make a line drawing on transparent tracing paper with a hard lead pencil.

2 To test an object for accuracy in a line drawing, fold the tracing (with wrong sides together) of the item in question in half, matching the right side of the object to the left side. Hold the tracing up to the light and compare the sides. If they don't match, erase the incorrect side and retrace it to match the side that looks correct.

3 Draw a line on the fold you just made through the center of the object. This is your vertical line. All vertical objects in your still life should be parallel to this line.

4 Take a clear graph ruler and align one of the vertical lines on the ruler to the vertical line drawn in step 3. Use the graph lines on your ruler to draw a horizontal line perpendicular to the vertical line. All horizontal objects in your still life should be parallel to this line.

5 You're now ready to transfer the design to the prepared surface. Align the vertical line parallel to the side of the surface and the horizontal line parallel to the bottom of the surface. Pay close attention to the details, as this is the only way to develop an accurate painting. Be certain to use good graphite (such as steno graphite) to apply the pattern.

Memories From Yesteryear

Surface Preparation

Seal the masonite panel with Designs From the Heart Wood Sealer. Apply a half-and-half basecoat mixture of Ceramcoat Lichen Grey + Queen Ann's Lace. Apply the first coat with either a sponge brush or Winsor & Newton Series 995 brush. Apply the second coat with a sponge roller brush (such as Pailard), which will give a surface that is ideal for dry-brush blending. The key to applying this finish is getting the right consistency of paint. Pour a small amount of the mixture on your disposable palette. Pick up the paint on your roller and apply in all directions. The paint will bubble on the masonite if it is too thin. If the paint is too thick, it will produce puddles or cavities. If you keep rolling the paint, both problems will correct themselves. If needed, you may wet sand with #400 or #600 sandpaper. Apply one very light coat of Krylon Matte Finish #1311 before applying the pattern. Be sure to read the section on Tips for Successfully Applying a Still-Life Design before transferring the pattern.

Mix the following colors on your palette:
Cool White – W + FU
Warm White – W + CYM
Warm Black – BU + FU
Cool Black – UB + BU

White China Bowl

Mix a warm black. Mix four values from dark to light by adding touches of warm black to W. These values will be used to create just enough value change to give the bowl its shape and dimension. The darkest mix will be your shading color, the next value will be the dark area, the next will be the middle value and the lightest will be the light area. The highlight will be warm white and the reflected light cool white. This will have to be built in stages. When you're pleased with the bowl, apply the pattern for the border. Because the border must follow the contour of the bowl, you will also need four values of the border color. Make these values with BC + NYH + NYR + NYL + W. The highlight will be warm white. When the border is dry, apply the small roses and leaves. Use the border mixture + W for the roses. The leaves are soft, greyed greens from the leaf mixtures of cool black + CYP + W. Once the roses and leaves are applied, they should be mopped with a mop brush to soften them into the border.

Memories From Yesteryear

Light-Value Grapes

Dark area	AC + BC + RS
Buff	CRL + NYH
Light area	CGP + NYH
Shade	Dark area mix + BU + (cool black)
Highlight	Light area mix + W + (CL) − W
Tint	W + Blk

Dark-Value Grapes

Base	AC + BC + RS + (DP)
Shade	Base mix + BU + (cool black)
Highlight	NY + NYR − (NYL)
Tint	W + Blk

Plums

Dark area	AC + BC + RS + (DP)
Buff	CRL + NYH
Light area	NYH + NYR
Shade	Dark area mix + BU + (cool black)
Highlight	NYR + NYL − W
Tint	W + Blk − CGP + YO

Leaves

Base	Cool black + CYM + (CGP) + (W)
Shade	Base mix + cool black
Highlight	W + CL − W + (CGP)
Tint	W + Blk − BC + RS

Blossom

Base	NYR + NY + NYL
Shade	BC + DP + RS + (cool black)
Highlight	NYL + CL + W − W
Tint	W + Blk

Burgundy Bottle

Dark area	BC + AC + BU
Light area	Dark area mix + NYH
Shade	Dark area mix + cool black
Highlight	NYR + NYL − (Dark area mix + cool white − W)
Tint	W + Blk

Cloth and Table

Use at least four values made from cool black + W and warm black + W. Pull a few burgundy tints into several areas. Shadows are done last with these same values.

Shadows

Shadows are generally the last thing applied to a painting, after it is dry. They do require time, thought and effort. Shadows become more beautiful and transparent if they are glazed on. The more times they are glazed, the greater their depth and sparkle.

Cast shadows are darker in value and cooler in temperature than the surface they are cast upon. The shadows in the foreground will be darker and sharper than shadows in the background. The color of the shadow should be neutral and complementary to the area the shadow is being cast upon. Objects in the direct line of the light source will cast darker and sharper shadows. The darkest value of the shadow falls where the subject comes in contact with the surface. As the shadow moves away from the subject, the value becomes lighter and the edge of the shadow becomes cooler. Some of the color of the subject creating the shadow will appear at the edge of the dark area (middle value) of the shadow.

The shape of the shadow follows the contour of the object that it is cast upon. Always work shadows that anchor an object to a surface parallel to the outside edge of the item the painting is on. A small amount of the cast shadow brought up onto the bottom of the subject will anchor the subject to the surface.

Conclusion

Creating and sharing the projects contained in this book has brought me a lot of pleasure. I hope they will bring you joy and satisfaction as you paint them.

My decorative painting career has been a wonderful journey, sometimes bumpy and full of questions, frustrations and feelings of failure. Yet also full of good times, love, wonderful friendships and fulfillment when that special painting is finished. I hope this book brings you a little further along the way on your journey. I urge you to understand the *why* be-hind the *how* of your painting, to question and explore new and different approaches. May your efforts produce the same satisfaction and fulfillment I have experienced.

If you aren't a member of the National Society of Tole and Decorative Painters, you are certainly missing out on a great experience. Contact the society at 393 North McLean Blvd., Wichita, KS 67203.

Happy Painting!

Index